Willa Cather
Writing at the Frontier

D0909239

Willa Cather in about 1902. Just back from her first trip abroad, she wears a pink satin Paris ball gown.

DISCARDED

DATE			
NOV 15 89			
APR 25			
MAY 17			
MY 31 '90			
5/4/93			
11/8/96			
12/2/96			

Berg Women's Series

Gertrude Bell	Susan Goodman
Mme de Staël	Renee Winegarten
Emily Dickinson	Donna Dickenson
Elizabeth Gaskell	Tessa Brodetsky
Mme du Châtelet	Esther Ehrmann
Emily Carr	Ruth Gowers
Simone de Beauvoir	Renee Winegarten
George Sand	Donna Dickenson
Sigrid Undset	Mitzi Brunsdale
Elizabeth I	Susan Bassnett
Margaret Fuller	David Watson

Volumes in preparation include

Edith Wharton	Valerie Shubik
Mary Anderson	Grenda Horne Hurt
Olive Schreiner	Ruth Gowers
Harriet Beecher Stowe	Lisa Watt MacFarlane

Willa Cather

Writing at the Frontier

Jamie Ambrose

BERG *Oxford/New York/Hamburg*

Distributed exclusively in the US and Canada by
St. Martin's Press, New York

Published in 1988 by
Berg Publishers Limited
77 Morrell Avenue, Oxford OX4 1NQ, UK
175 Fifth Avenue/Room 400, New York, NY 10010, USA
Nordalbingerweg 14, 2000 Hamburg 61, FRG

British Library Cataloguing in Publication Data

Ambrose, Jamie
  Willa Cather. — (Berg women's series).
  1. Cather, Willa. — Biography
  2. Novelists, American — 20th century
  — Biography
  I. Title
  813'.52   PS3505.A87Z/

  ISBN 0–85496–152–6

Library of Congress Cataloging-in-Publication Data

Ambrose, Jamie.
  Willa Cather/Jamie Ambrose.
      p.   cm. — (Berg women's series)
  Bibliography: p.
  Includes index.
  ISBN 0–85496–152–6: $22.50 (U.S.)
  1. Cather, Willa, 1873–1947 — Criticism and interpretation.
I. Title.   II. Series.
PS3505.A87Z55   1988
813'.52 — dc 19   87–29969

Printed in Great Britain by Billings of Worcester

For my parents

Contents

Illustrations

The author and publishers are grateful to the Nebraska State Historical Society for permission to reproduce Plates 1–9.

Acknowledgements

Most of the works of Willa Cather are protected by copyright. Quotations from *O Pioneers!*, *My Ántonia* and *The Song of the Lark* are reproduced by permission of Houghton Mifflin (US) and the Virago Press (UK). For permission to quote from *April Twilights*, *The Kingdom of Art*, *The World and the Parish*, and Mildred Bennett's *The World of Willa Cather* I am indebted to the University of Nebraska Press. All other Cather quotations are reproduced by permission of Alfred A. Knopf Inc., as are those from Edith Lewis's *Willa Cather Living* and E. K. Brown's *Willa Cather: A Critical Biography*.

Throughout the writing of this book I have incurred a number of debts of gratitude to individuals: to Mildred R. Bennett, for her generosity and assistance with photographs; to Lucia Woods Lindley, for the use of her beautiful photograph 'Virgin Prairie'; to the staff of the British Library, for their assistance. I would also like to express my deep gratitude to the following: first and foremost, to my publisher, Dr Marion Berghahn, for her guidance, encouragement and endless forbearance; to my editors, Juliet Standing and Janet Godden, for hard work and patience; to Ina Mende, for assistance with research; to Dr Gerald Rainer, who first started me on this path; to EJ, for perennial confidence; and to DAH, for good advice and the use of the *sanctum sanctorum*.

Jamie Ambrose
June 1988

'To work in silence and with all one's heart, that is the writer's lot; he is the only artist who must be a solitary, and yet needs the widest outlook upon the world.'

Letter of Sarah Orne Jewett to Willa Cather,
13 December 1908

'The talent for writing is largely the talent for living. . . . There is only one way to see the world truly, and that is to see it in a human way.'

From an article in *The Nebraska State Journal*,
28 October 1894

Preface

> When a writer once begins to work with his own material, he realizes that, no matter what his literary excursions may have been, he has been working with it from the beginning — by living it.
>
> from Preface to *Alexander's Bridge*

Willa Cather was born in 1873 into the structured society of nineteenth-century Virginia. She spent the later years of her childhood in the very different environment of the Nebraska plains — an experience, she later claimed, that shocked open her awareness. After a university education, in the course of which she published essays, short stories and newspaper columns, she moved to the East coast to support herself as a journalist, at the same time developing her literary talents. While she was writing as a newspaperwoman, a magazine editor and a critic, therefore, Cather was also experimenting with and exploring the principles of creativity through poetry and short stories. When at last she turned her attention to the novel this exploration continued to reflect the pattern of her life, finding different avenues and means of expression, revealing the ever-changing process of a creative mind.

Since her death in 1947, the amount of attention devoted to Willa Cather and her writing has been both wide-ranging and exhaustive. From E.K. Brown's initial biography to the most recent feminist studies, scholars, critics and friends have sought to define her life and classify her art, to arrive at the definitive interpretation, the complete portrait of one of America's most original and enduring writers.

The task has not been an easy one because of the nature of the subject herself. The world at large knows her as a prize-winning novelist, but that is only the tip of the professional iceberg. Before the appearance of her first novel *Alexander's Bridge* in 1912, Willa Cather had served a long apprenticeship as essayist, art critic, journalist, short-story writer and editor — and much of this work had appeared either anonymously or under one of a bewildering variety of pseudonyms.

To further complicate matters, Cather herself was increasingly reluctant to discuss herself or her writing. She destroyed much of her correspondence, forbade publication of the rest and, after one encounter with the film world, fiercely resisted all attempts to dramatize her work for the media. Her early experiments with fiction she either ignored completely or dismissed as studio work; her private life and her copyrights were guarded tenaciously, with only a few selections of each presented for public viewing. Had this 'official' portrait remained unchallenged, Cather would certainly have remained a literary enigma.

Happily, such is not now the case. Her reticence only served to stimulate research and thanks to the efforts of such scholars as Mildred Bennett, Bernice Slote, Virginia Faulkner and William Curtin, much of the mystery surrounding Cather's early years has been removed and the vast bulk of previously unknown and uncollected writing is now available to the public. The result has been a far more realistic and interesting portrait of the author than she would ever have allowed.

'The portrait of a great artist, as it finally emerges, must come, I think, from many sources and from many minds.' Thus Cather's friend and close companion, Edith Lewis, wrote so aptly of the writer she had known for over forty years. 'I have written about Willa Cather as I knew her,' Miss Lewis continued, 'but with the feeling that it is not in any form of biological writing, but in art alone, that the deepest truth about human beings is to be found.'

There are probably few writers to whom such an assertion applies in the same degree as it does to Willa Cather. From the first passionate essays to the more reserved manuscripts of later years, her work is filled with a personal intensity, characterized by a quality of voice that is hers and hers alone. Taken as a whole — and including the instances in which that voice is immature or masked by 'literary' writing (a bad word in Cather's vocabulary) — Willa Cather's writing can be seen as an embodiment, a mirror of the artist's life. Her life and art were so intertwined, indeed, that at times not even she could tell them apart.

My intention in offering yet another study of Cather has been to provide some sort of introduction to this interweaving; by making use of Miss Lewis's many minds and sources I hope to point the reader towards some of the deeper truths in Cather's works. My approach is through the sympathy I feel for this artist, as a younger writer to an older, greater one who yet shares a similar background. Like Cather, I was born in the South and at a similar age experienced the shock of being planted in a very different environment. Like her, I am a single woman making my way in the world through writing. These are my own apprentice years of journalism, where her Pittsburgh has become my London. I hope that sharing this common ground has enabled me to bring out certain points that other biographers may have missed. I have also drawn on the accounts of Cather written by those who knew her (chiefly Edith Lewis and Elizabeth Shepley Sergeant), on the factual basis provided by the sound scholarship of Bennett, Brown, Slote, Woodress and others, and on the writings of Cather herself, which have provided me with a close and constant guidance.

Some readers may question why I, as a woman writer, have not attempted to turn a more feminist spotlight on my subject. I would answer them by saying that here I have felt guided by Cather herself. She was not interested in such analysis of art and artists; neither did she have a high opinion of the feminists of her day, such as the suffragettes. She simply got on with life and accomplished her aims. While she was undoubtedly irritated by some of her society's attitudes to women, this never impeded her in her chosen course. I therefore feel justified in presenting such a life as hers as its own best explanation. Mention should be made, however, of the excellent current Virago editions of Cather's novels, which contain some thought-provoking essays by A.S. Byatt; also a recent study of particular interest to those who wish to follow a more overtly feminist approach to Cather is Sharon O'Brien's *Willa Cather: The Emerging Voice* which tackles the question of Cather's possible lesbianism.

Willa Cather left as her legacy some of the finest works of American literature; through her writings she also gave us a personal chronicle of artistic development. 'Every artist makes himself born,' Harsanyi tells Thea Kronborg in *The Song of the Lark*. 'It is very much harder than the other time, and longer.' For Willa Cather, it lasted until the day of her death.

1 First Impressions

> I think that most of the basic material a writer
> works with is acquired before the age of fifteen. . . .
> Those years determine whether one's work will be
> poor and thin or rich and fine.

Willa Cather, in an interview with Latrobe Carroll, 1921

Willa Cather had initially extended her line of demarcation from
fifteen to twenty, the age at which she began to write for the
Nebraska State Journal. Her implication, however, is clear enough:
the early years are formative ones. Both Cather and the rest of the
world later placed greater emphasis on the latter half of her
childhood; but the psychological and linguistic studies of the last
two decades have only just begun to show the dramatic effects
environment has upon the mind from its earliest beginnings.
Willa Cather would have hated such an approach, believing that
art should never be analysed. The origins of art can never be fully
explained, but the origins of life may take us closer to its truths.

The world knew her as 'Miss Willa Cather from Nebraska'.
Indeed, anyone reading *O Pioneers!*, *My Ántonia*, or a myriad of
short stories would naturally assume that the author had cut her
teeth on the red Nebraska plains. But when a daughter was born
to Charles and Virginia Cather in December 1873, the birthplace
was not the rough country of the Divide. Instead, Willa Cather's
first personal setting was that of the Shenandoah Valley of
Virginia.

Traditionally, Cather's Virginia years are treated in terms of
individuals — the first people with whom the child came in
contact, their effects upon her, how they emerged in her fiction. I
intend also to discuss them in this fashion. Initially, however, I
wish to touch on the effect the society had upon the writer, a point
that is sometimes overlooked.

Is it coincidence that Cather, to whom the past meant so much,
spent the first years of her life in the oldest of all the United
States? Virginia's history is dazzling by US standards — John
Smith landed there in 1607; the first colonists arrived in 1609.

1

With the introduction of slaves and indentured servants, a mini-aristocracy soon developed, and by the latter half of the eighteenth century even the wilder Shenandoah region had been more or less civilised. Virginia was home to a host of presidents and Revolutionary and Civil War heroes: Washington, Jefferson, Madison and Monroe; Patrick Henry; all the Lees, from Richard Henry down to the Confederate General Robert E. By the time Cather was born, Virginia as a settled area was well over 200 years old. The state possessed a tradition of history which not only linked it with the Old World across the ocean, but also made it the Old World of America itself.

It is not possible to grow up in any part of the South without being aware of history. Cather certainly would have been exposed to Virginia's heritage as a child, through the stories of her own family and others gleaned from neighbours and visitors. She always said that the old immigrant women of Nebraska gave her the first 'real feeling of an older world across the sea', and that claim is not to be disputed. But the *idea* of that older world's existence had surely been planted in her consciousness long before she arrived in Nebraska.

If Virginia gave Cather a sense of the past and of an older order, it also placed her on common ground with those same pioneer immigrants in their homesickness for lands left behind them. And surely the Southern ways which surrounded Cather from birth — the leisurely pace, the enjoyment of food and drink, the delight in stories — must have propelled her towards her strange fellow exiles, whose methods were similar, yet intriguingly different; the *Ursprung*, in part, of her own. It therefore seems reasonable to surmise that the Virginia background played a greater part in directing and moulding the young author than is generally allowed.

Of course as Cather would write in *O Pioneers!*, 'the history of every country begins in the heart of a man or a woman'. Southerners in general and Virginians in particular are noted for their obsession with genealogy; history becomes personal, sprinkled throughout with family figures. The Cathers were no different from other Southerners and preserved a wealth of material concerning family origins. Willa Cather knew the family stories herself, and because her immediate relatives figured so prominently in her works it is worth examining the Cather ancestry.

Cathers had been present in the Shenandoah Valley since colonial times. Tradition points to Welsh origins; the surname may have been derived from Cader Idris, the dominating mountain near the supposed ancestral home. Another legend tells of a distant relative fighting for Charles I and of twin brothers rewarded with an Irish land grant by Charles II. At any rate, Jasper, the first recorded Cather, came to the New World from Ireland sometime before the American War of Independence, eventually settling in the Shenandoah Valley.

His grandson William is the next Cather of importance. By 1851 William Cather had established the farm he called Willow Shade near the village of Back Creek Valley, Frederick County, Virginia (Back Creek has since become present-day Gore). The traits of nonconformity, will-power, and determination are evident in his personality, just as they are in that of his famous granddaughter. This zealous man had already provoked familial disapproval by embracing the Baptist Church at a time when all Cathers were Calvinists, but the greatest breach of conduct was yet to come. When the Civil War broke out in 1861 William sided with the North; Willow Shade was even used as a meeting point for Union troops. While this decision severed William's family ties for many years, it also ensured his financial stability.

By the end of the war — a time when most Southerners were bankrupt — Willow Shade encompassed over 300 acres of land, including the spacious three-storey house of the same name. Because he had escaped the war's backlash, William Cather continued to earn a comfortable living from the sale of sheep to the Maryland markets (the land was too rocky to raise much else). Their Union sympathies notwithstanding, the Cathers maintained good relations with their neighbours in Back Creek Valley; it was William who hired a county school-teacher when no other man could afford to do so.

William's wife was Emily Anne Caroline Smith, a lady whose English ancestry was no less interesting than her husband's Celtic origins. One forebear had received land grants from the Baron of Cameron, Lord Fairfax, in 1762. Any event or personage which made an impression on Willa Cather was almost certain to emerge at some point in her fiction, and this ancestral story was no exception. The Smith family link with the Old World forms the subject of an early short story, 'A Night In

Greenway Court' (1896). There is also reference to the Fairfax connection in *Sapphira and the Slave Girl* (1940), itself the result of family history and the only novel Cather set in Virginia.

People, however, were Cather's main concern, even as a child. It is accepted that the Cather grandparents are portrayed in Josiah and Emmaline Burden, the grandparents of orphaned Jim in *My Ántonia* (1918). Here William appears as he was in life: blue-eyed and bald, with a beard remarkable for its texture and whiteness (see plate 2). Willa, speaking through 'Jim', found him impressive and dignified — and not a little frightening because of his stern Baptist disposition. Caroline/Emmaline seems to have been more approachable, characterised by energy and the high, nervous laugh which accompanies her 'lively intelligence' (see plate 1). Although well on in years by the time they moved to Nebraska, the William Cathers still possessed the vitality necessary to raise three orphaned grandchildren, offspring of two daughters who had died of tuberculosis.

Their roles in *Ántonia* aside, neither William nor Caroline Cather seems to have touched their granddaughter with deep, real feeling — presumably because her early life was not so closely connected with theirs. It was Rachel Seibert Boak, Cather's maternal grandmother, who left a more profound impression on young Willa's life. It may also have been she who first instilled in Willa Cather the quality of sympathy that is so characteristic of her works.

Rachel Seibert, also of Back Creek Valley, married William Boak, a Virginia delegate and official in the Department of the Interior in Washington, DC. After his early death, the young widow and her five children returned to her Virginia home, not far from Willow Shade Farm. Mrs Boak's house, a gift from her father, became the birthplace of Willa Cather (see plate 3).

Cather's conception of her grandmother as a young woman may be seen in *Sapphira and the Slave Girl*. In this novel Rachel Blake, also a young widow, rebels against her mother's tradition of slavery by helping a Negro girl escape to freedom — Rachel Boak had done the same. Mrs Blake spends her time helping the mountain poor, tending the sick, making a frugal living for herself and her children. Although only in her thirties (as Mrs Boak was), she seems much older, moving through the days with a grave determination.

4

Nowhere, however, is Rachel Boak more sensitively portrayed than in 'Old Mrs. Harris' (1932), a short story that Edith Lewis thought could easily have been called 'Family Portraits'. Cather's remarkable memory and descriptive powers are well in evidence throughout this story, which was written over thirty years after her grandmother's death.

'Mrs. Harris' shows the Cather family in their early years in Red Cloud, cramped into a house much too small for them and not yet fully adjusted to the strange ways of a Western town. As 'Mrs Harris', Grandmother Boak possesses an 'intensely quiet dignity' derived from her 'complete resignation to the chances of life'. No doubt resignation was vital when accepting a 'chance' that had uprooted her from a comfortable Southern home and placed her in constricting and unfamiliar surroundings. Her warm, gentle eyes 'seemed to ask nothing and hope for nothing', yet she is not necessarily a pathetic creature: 'there was the kind of nobility about her head that there is about an old lion's'. Even her mouth Cather describes as 'composed' or 'resigned', a mouth which never smiled — though when her grandchildren were tumbling about her like so many puppies, she 'looked happy'.

Rachel Boak also possessed an enquiring mind. 'Grandmother loved to read, anything at all', Cather writes of Mrs Harris, for the same was true of her own grandmother. Grandmother Boak began Willa's education, reading to her from such books as *The Pilgrim's Progress*, the Bible and *Peter Parley's Universal History*. Not unexpectedly, the *History* proved a favourite of Willa's; as a toddler, she evidently spent a great deal of time driving a make-believe chariot through ancient Rome, while an invisible slave ran alongside her shouting, 'Cato, thou art but man!' As she grew older, it was Willa who read to Mrs Boak.

Cather's sympathetic portrayal of older people — particularly older women — would seem to be largely a result of her close relationship with Mrs Boak. It was probably another factor which drew her to those first elderly foreigners of the Divide. Rachel Boak was separated from her own traditions and methods of coping with life — a separation no less cruel because it was unavoidable. Time and again we see Cather's heroes and heroines respecting the rights of the old to retain their own ways: Alexandra with little Mrs Lee (*O Pioneers!*), Claude with Mahailey (*One of Ours*). Cather seems to have been guilt-ridden for not having recognised her grandmother's plight sooner than she did. By assuming fictional guise as 'Vickie' in 'Old Mrs. Harris', Cather criticises herself almost to the point of brutality, juxtaposing the oblivious self-absorption of youth with the secret sufferings of Grandmother Harris.

There were two even more prominent individuals in Cather's heart and mind (or, her art and life). Throughout her life the writer drew unceasingly and, in many cases, unconsciously upon the figures of her own parents.

Charles Fectigue Cather married Mary Virginia Boak, Rachel's daughter, in 1872. Charles Cather (see plate 6) was by all accounts both handsome and a gentleman: 'tall, fair-haired, and blue-eyed, with extremely gentle, courteous manners'. As Hilary Templeton in 'Old Mrs. Harris', his boyish face and polite Southern ways 'made him appear very soft to some of the hard old money-grubbers' of a Nebraska town; one can imagine how odd Mr Cather's soft 'yes, sir', or 'no, ma'am', would have sounded among the other Western accents. Willa Cather also seems to have made her father the subject of an early *Nebraska State Journal* vignette: 'He was a Virginian and a gentleman and for that reason he was fleeced on every side . . . it does not pay to be a Southern gentleman in the hustling Northwest.' One can taste the bitterness in these lines, written when Cather was twenty.

Charles Cather must have lacked both the zeal and the iron will of his father and his brother George. He appears to have been infinitely better suited to the less aggressive life style of the South than to the rough ways of pioneer Nebraska. That his daughter loved him is evident in her works; it is also clear that — at least on the surface — he assumed the more passive role in his marriage. This is not to suggest that he was henpecked; he simply left the control of domestic affairs in the hands of his wife.

Possibly he never had another option, for Virginia Boak Cather (see plate 5) was a match for any man. A striking woman, she was charming, hospitable, and somewhat imperious in the running of her household. It was Virginia who healed the rift in the Cather clan (due to Grandfather William's Union loyalties) by inviting all the estranged members to a reunion at Willow Shade. This same Southern belle also disciplined her children with a rawhide whip, just as Mrs Kronborg does in *The Song of the Lark* (1915). But like Mrs Kronborg, Mrs Cather also 'let her children's minds alone . . . respected them as individuals, and outside of the house, they had a great deal of liberty'.

Used to an active social life and the special treatment of women the South afforded, Virginia Cather was as much out of place in the West as her mother. Again we can turn to 'Old Mrs. Harris' for Cather's summation of her. Victoria Templeton is fastidious in her appearance and both self-centred and generous. Warm and genuine, Victoria 'had a good heart, but she was terribly proud and could not bear the least criticism'. Willa Cather believed herself to resemble her mother in temperament, and it may be assumed that the two personalities often clashed. But it was due to Virginia Cather's insight that Willa went to college; Charles had vaguely assumed that his daughter would probably teach a little after high school.

Is it any wonder that the majority of Cather's maternal characters appear strong, well-defined, and dominant? The Kronborg, Templeton and Colbert mothers all command the respect, if not necessarily the love, of their children. When married couples are portrayed wives usually retain the upper hand, as in *My Mortal Enemy* (1926) or *The Professor's House* (1925). Love — the purely adoring kind — seems reserved for Cather's fathers, with a good deal of frustration thrown in. They are generally physically attractive, yet their personal characteristics are not clear. Notoriously vague, they drift in and out of the pages almost without trace. The reader senses that they are both loved and loving but so distanced from their children's lives that they are often unaware of their abilities; the ones who are aware die early in the stories. The one notable exception to both these arguments is *One of Ours* (1922), in which the Wheeler parents seem to be loosely modelled on Cather's Aunt Franc and Uncle George.

This, then, was the immediate family circle into which Willa Cather was born on 7 December 1873. She was christened 'Wilella', probably for an aunt who had died in childhood, but her family usually called her 'Willie'. 'Willa' must have been her own invention, for she altered the name herself in the family Bible. At the time of their daughter's birth the Charles Cathers were living with Rachel Boak in Back Creek Valley, some thirteen miles west of Winchester, Virginia.

Charles's brother George and his wife Frances had left Willow Shade before Willa's birth, the first of the family to venture westward. In 1874 William Cather paid an extended visit to his elder son in Nebraska, leaving Charles to run the farm; accordingly, Charles moved his little family, including Rachel Boak, to Willow Shade. It was to be Willa Cather's home for the next eight years, and the birthplace of her brothers Roscoe and Douglass and her sister Jessica; three other siblings — James, Elsie, and John ('Jack') — were born in Nebraska. This sprawling, rocky farm became the stuff of Cather's earliest memories.

The house itself was a typical Southern *antebellum*: a large brick affair with traditional fluted columns. There were green shutters at the windows, and each room had its own fireplace. A mountain spring supplied the house with running water and a small creek ran through the front yard. Great willow trees adorned the grounds — hence the name — and a box hedge connected the colonnade at the front entrance with the creek below. Situated along the turnpike from Winchester to Romney the house, which appears in the epilogue of *Sapphira*, was never cut off from the outside world. The climate of the valley was also agreeable; the Cathers escaped both the paralysing heat of summer and the freezing winter winds. High humidity, however, did create an atmosphere of damp, a factor which is believed to have influenced the family to move west; damp was thought to contribute to tuberculosis, and the Cather family seemed prone to the disease.

Friends and relatives often visited at Willow Shade; there was also a steady stream of travelling pedlars and salesmen. The Cathers had never been slave-owners, but both black and white servants bustled through the house, together with various 'mountain women' — poorer neighbours from the hills who came in periodically to help with quilting, canning, soap-making or other chores. There were certainly no feelings of isolation at Willow Shade.

In addition to Grandmother Boak and the growing number of children, another member of the Cather household was Margie Anderson. Margie was a poor, rather simple mountain girl who served the family as nurse and housemaid, and who accompanied them to Nebraska. Willa Cather's sympathies were also extended to people such as Margie. She is the 'Mandy' of 'Old Mrs. Harris', the 'Mahailey' of *One of Ours*, and the subject of 'Poor Marty', a poem published in the *Atlantic Monthly* in 1931. Although Margie was illiterate Cather recognised in her a different kind of wisdom: Margie was an instinctive judge of character.

Mary Ann Anderson, Margie's mother, also left an impression on the young Willa. She was just the type of character Cather loved to be around, both as a child and as an adult. When she visited Virginia in later life, Mrs Anderson was never forgotten. She may be found in the 'Mrs Ringer' of *Sapphira*, uneducated but interested in everything and everyone, up on all the local gossip and full of tales — a forerunner of those foreign story-tellers of the Divide.

Cather's early childhood was filled by soft-spoken people, their dialogues and anecdotes. Food and conversation in the South are simply excuses one for the other, and it is easy to picture the child Willa sitting in some out-of-the-way spot after supper, listening while the drowsy sound of a variety of Southern voices washed over and around her. Certainly it was through writing about Nebraska and the people of the plains that Willa Cather first established her name and made some of her greatest contributions to literature. It was absolutely necessary that a woman of her temperament 'escape' the South; for all its charms it can smother creative people, restricting them by its comfort and its altered sense of time. The South can be mesmerising; yet it can also instil in one a real interest in people, stories, and the past. I believe that the Virginia years contributed much more towards Cather's capacity for caring about people than she would admit, as well as developing her interest in history. Life in a Southern household would have trained the child to listen, because there was so much to listen to — as may be seen in *Sapphira and the Slave Girl*.

Sapphira is based on a true story, and the author herself witnessed the reunion of the ex-slave, Nancy, with her mother Old Till. Cather was five years old at the time and later recounted the scene in full: 'Till had already risen; when the stranger followed my mother into the room, she took a few uncertain steps forward. She fell meekly into the arms of a tall, gold-skinned woman, who drew the little old darky to her breast and held her there . . . There was something Scriptural in that meeting, like the pictures in our old Bible.'

During the rest of Nancy's stay Willa characteristically tagged along after Till and her daughter, staying just as close as she was able, listening to every word: 'Sometimes their talk was puzzling, but I soon learned that it was best never to interrupt with questions, — it seemed to break the spell. Nancy wanted to know what had happened during the war, and what had become of everybody, — and so did I.'

'Ah, it is things like that, which haunt the mind for years, and at last write themselves down, that belong, whether little or great, to literature.' Willa Cather was quoting her friend and mentor, Sarah Orne Jewett, during an interview given in 1913. Many incidents haunted Cather throughout her lifetime. Yet is it coincidence that *Sapphira*, though by no means her best work, was the last novel she completed? A little incident, a Southern incident, but one which haunted her for over sixty years.

2 The Beginnings of Awareness

> . . . they had all, like Ántonia, been early awakened
> and made observant by coming at a tender age from
> an old country to a new.
>
> *My Ántonia*

The Civil War left America reeling with shock and shame. In
1776 the country had been founded upon the ideals of freedom
and right of choice; less than ninety years later it was torn apart
for the sake of those same ideals. In the years following the war
the United States, desperate to shift attention from its incestuous
feud, found salvation in one word: expansion.

The early nineteenth century had seen explorers and adventurers such as John C. Frémont and Kit Carson blazing the trails
westward. They were followed in the 1840s by pioneers of the
great Mormon migrations and the 'forty-niners' of the California
gold rush. Immediately after the Civil War, however, the wagon
trails were replaced by miles of iron track, and in 1869 the first
transcontinental railroad, the Union Pacific, was completed; at
about the same time the Burlington railroad entered Nebraska at
Platsmouth. Cheap land, low interest rates, hope for a better
future, and now improved transportation . . . all meshed to form
an irresistible magnet. When the cry went up to 'Go West!',
Americans and immigrants alike responded in droves.

It is not known exactly what caused the Cathers to leave the
state which had been their home for generations. The new
frontier meant a new start for many bankrupt Southerners, yet
the Cathers did not share their neighbours' plight. There has
been some speculation as to possible local enmity caused by
William's Northern sympathies; this is also highly unlikely. Even
if it were true, William Cather was not a man to run from trouble,
to allow his neighbours to 'hate him out'.

A more plausible explanation is the high incidence of tuberculosis in the family. Four of William's brothers had died of TB; his
daughters were ill with it and he himself was not in good health.
It is likely that, during his visit to George Cather in Nebraska, he

found the semi-arid climate helpful to his condition. Whatever the reason, he bought some land there. When he and Caroline returned to Virginia it was only to settle their affairs, collect a widowed daughter, and return to Nebraska permanently in 1877. The daughter, Jennie Cather Ayres, survived the journey, but died soon afterwards; the poem 'Macon Prairie' recalls her courageous spirit.

When a fire destroyed Willow Shade's four-storey barn, Charles Cather decided to sell the property and join his parents and brother. In February 1883 the farm and equipment were auctioned for $6,000, and the Cathers set off for south-central Nebraska, arriving at the town of Red Cloud in Webster County. Besides Charles, Virginia, and the four children, the party which stepped off the Burlington train included Rachel Boak, Margie Anderson and her brother, and two cousins.

For the first eighteen months Willa Cather's new home was her grandfather's house on the plains (he had returned to Virginia for a visit, and Grandmother Cather moved in with George and Frances). 'Catherton', as the settlement was already known, lay about sixteen miles north-west of Red Cloud in the country between the Blue and Republican rivers known as the Divide. When George and Frances Cather arrived to claim their tract of land, they had had no idea where it was located; all the country looked the same and there were few, if any, natural boundaries or markers. These Cather pioneers had estimated the distance from Red Cloud by measuring the circumference of a wagon wheel, tying a rag to its rim, then counting the revolutions and reckoning accordingly.

That the world Willa Cather encountered at the age of nine was called 'the Divide' is almost too appropriate. Nebraska was the complete antithesis of Virginia: miles upon miles of grassland, a country which magnified all of life's contrasts by its sheer barrenness. It was also a country that marked the division of Cather's childhood into two distinct periods.

At that time Nebraska was indeed the 'newest part of the New World'. It had gained statehood in 1867, only six years before Willa Cather's birth; Red Cloud itself was just fourteen years old when she first set foot there. Although the Cathers came to Nebraska in the midst of the boom years of immigration, most of the country around Red Cloud was still virgin prairie. Out on the

Divide, one's nearest neighbours might be three or four miles away, usually in either a dugout or a sod house (the prairie soil was so tightly bound by matted grass roots that chunks could be cut and lifted for use as building bricks).

Native Americans were rare among the prairie folk. During the 1860s and 1870s the Nebraska State Board of Immigration had employed an agent in Europe whose business it was to attract immigrants. The handbill campaigns of the Burlington and Union Pacific railroads brought in even greater numbers of foreigners. Of these, Germany supplied the largest amount, followed by Sweden and the other Scandinavian countries; then Bohemia, Prussia, and the British Isles. Like Willa Cather, these people were totally unprepared for their new land; the handbills had not described the sight which met their eyes.

The prairie stretched out before them, unbroken in all directions. The long, dry grass, undulating in the wind, made the country seem like some vast, reddish-brown sea. The Indians, like the buffalo before them, had either been driven out or subdued, and the Divide was left to the coyotes, jackrabbits, prairie dogs, rattlesnakes and other animals of the plains. In the days before irrigation, water was scarce, used only for cooking and drinking; a bath was a miracle. Trees were things to be preserved and worshipped. Nebraska's ruthless climate made life especially difficult for early settlers such as Cather's Aunt Franc. The hot winds of summer pushed the mercury in the thermometers above 90° or even 100°F; in winter temperatures plunged well below zero. Blizzards were to be expected. It was a land of harsh beauty which demanded much from those coming to meet it.

Willa Cather never forgot the shock of her own first encounter. To a child used to the security of mountains and woodlands, that initial vision of naked prairie must have been terrifying. She recalled her reaction in *My Ántonia*, speaking through Jim as he peers out of the wagon carrying him to his grandparents:

> There was nothing but land . . . I had the feeling that the world was left behind, that we had got over the edge of it, and were outside man's jurisdiction. I had never before looked up at the sky when there was not a familiar mountain ridge against it . . . this was the complete dome of heaven. . . . Between that earth and that sky I felt erased, blotted out.

These are but echoes of an oft-quoted interview Cather gave in 1913:

> I was sitting on the hay in the bottom of a Studebaker wagon, holding on to the side of the wagon box to steady myself. . . . As we drove further and further out into the country, I felt a good deal as if we had come to the end of everything — it was a kind of erasure of personality. I would not know how much a child's life is bound up in the woods and hills and meadows around it, if I had not been jerked away from all these and thrown into a country as bare as a piece of sheet iron.

In the following passage, Cather's perception of beauty has already been awakened by the stark new land:

> I had heard my father say you had to show grit in a new country, and I would have got on pretty well if it had not been for the larks. Every now and then one flew up and sang a few splendid notes and dropped down into the grass again. That reminded me of something — I don't know what, but my one purpose in life just then was not to cry, and every time they did it, I thought I should go under.

It is worth asking, however, how much these interview stories are based on actual fact. Cather was as notoriously selective in her memories as she was in her way of seeing. Her imagination was such that it often invented happenings that she, consciously or otherwise, treated as fact. What is clear is that the child responded to her new country with feeling from the very beginning. Initially it was the hate spawned by homesickness. Gradually, she and the land 'had it out together'. She would say that by the autumn of 1883, the Divide held her in its grip: 'It has been the happiness and the curse of my life'.

The Cathers were more fortunate than most in Webster County: a house awaited them upon their arrival, a proper one, built of wood. Adjustment was none the less difficult. Virginia Cather was often taken ill (no doubt partly from homesickness), and young Willa was left to herself much of the time.

Not that she minded; there was so much to explore in this new world. Alone or with her playmates, the Lambrechts, Cather soon uncovered the beauty of the prairie (plate 10). She investigated the ravines, or 'draws', hunted for prairie-dog towns, searched for the old buffalo wallows — still extant, even though the animals themselves were gone. Sometimes she went snake hunting. She said that she gathered the various wild flowers in great heaps, and wept over them: 'They were so lovely, and no one seemed to care for them at all!' Cather remained passionately fond of flowers throughout her life.

As always, however, it was the human element that mattered most; she wrote later that the people of the Divide stood out even more brilliantly than its flowers, 'like daubs of color on a painter's palette'. As the young Willa rode about the plains, exploring or running errands for her family, her natural curiosity caused her to seek out these interesting foreign neighbours, many of whom spoke few words of English. They fascinated her and she liked them straightaway, especially the older women who understood her own homesickness. In spite of the language barriers, they managed to tell the girl many stories from their homelands, filling the places of people like Mary Ann Anderson.

Cather was incensed that her own family did not seem to share her enthusiasm for the immigrants. Americans in general, she believed, were rarely fair in their judgements of the Europeans among them. New Englanders kept as far away as possible from the 'foreigners', while Southerners, though always ready to lend a hand in times of trouble, were 'provincial and utterly without curiosity'. Being a child, however, gave Cather an advantage she did not understand, or always admit. Earlier, she had acknowledged that the immigrants felt more at ease with a child, telling her more than would ever have been revealed to an adult. Even as a child, Cather was preternaturally receptive:

> I have never found any intellectual excitement any more intense that I used to feel when I spent a morning with one of these old women at her baking or butter making. I used to ride home in the most unreasonable state of excitement; I always felt as if they told me so much more than they said — as if I had actually got inside another person's skin.

Before her conscious conceptions of art began to form, Willa Cather's awareness had been deeply touched by two things: a new landscape and the immigrants who settled in it. The seemingly endless, empty plains of the American Midwest can provide an overwhelming experience to newcomers more used to the reduced scale of the southern States or a European homeland. But what could so 'excite' a child about old women at their daily tasks? As first-born, Willa had been constantly in the company of people older than herself. The special relationship with Mrs Boak has been noted, as well as the unconscious implantation of a sense of the past. What was unique about the immigrant settlers for Cather was that they *were* the past. The old women were not words, or tales, or the pages of a book. They came, living, from the Old World, and turned the stories into reality. Here were people who had been born in countries far across the sea, who had breathed another air. They spoke a different language, they wore strange garments; even their smell was different — exotic. Some had brought with them a few treasured possessions from the far-off lands: small pieces of furniture, a violin, dried mushrooms. Such things were not lost on Willa Cather.

More important, the immigrants brought their traditions. The old hands that Willa saw kneading dough represented generations of technique. They were patient hands, performing everyday tasks from a long tradition of care and love. Sometimes, of course, this very tradition became the downfall of the immigrants, when they tried to farm a new land with old techniques. For those who could not adapt, at least partially, failure, starvation, even death usually followed. Some of the stories Willa heard during bread baking were present tales of tragedy, such as the suicide of Francis Sadilek, alias 'Papa Shimerda' of *My Ántonia*. It was because of such sudden contrasts that Willa Cather's writing became fraught with the juxtaposition of opposites. Such opposing forces also emphasised the brevity of existence, deepening Cather's concern for little things — particularly time-worn methods and material, which could be swept away in an instant. Before ever seeing a play or hearing a concert, Willa Cather had come to love the little, peaceful arts, the beautiful crafts of everyday living.

Intellect was not neglected for feeling. Indeed, Cather was fortunate in her family, however, 'provincial' she considered them to be at times. There are some 'Cather legends' surrounding her early life on the Divide. They picture a young girl riding wild across the prairie, unlearned, imbibing her stories from the soil like some 'natural artist'. This was no more true of Willa Cather than it was of Robert Burns. Her institutional schooling had, until now, been neglected; the new school at Catherton provided tuition for only three months of the year. But despite this lack of formal education, Willa had been learning all along from a variety of teachers.

Grandmother Boak remained an important influence. Now, however, it was Willa who did the reading, and from sources other than the Bible. They spent many evenings together, reading Shakespeare, Ben Johson and Byron. As the eldest, Willa was often called upon to read to her younger siblings; she certainly knew *The Swiss Family Robinson*, *The Arabian Nights*, and the tales of the Brothers Grimm. Charles Cather was also in the habit of reading to the family. Some of his favourites were Matthew Arnold's *Sohrab and Rustum*, and the poems of Thomas Moore and Thomas Campbell.

Another of Cather's teachers was her beloved Aunt Franc, otherwise Frances H. Smith, the wife of George Cather. Aunt Franc was another incongruous figure on the frontier; a Massachusetts girl, she had been educated at Mount Holyoke Female Seminary, one of the earliest New England colleges for women. In addition to raising five children and running a pioneer household, Frances Cather managed to organise a Sunday school and arrange 'literaries', or cultural evenings held in various households. She also found time to spend with her young niece. 'The good old lady told me stories till she grew quite young again', Cather recalled in a Pittsburgh column. Those stories concerned discussions of Frances Cather's favourite authors, including Keats, Shelley, Byron, and Moore; also American transcendentalists such as Ralph Waldo Emerson. Frances Cather was also musically inclined, if we accept her portrait as 'Aunt Georgiana' in 'A Wagner Matinee' (1904).

Aunt Georgiana is a figure to be pitied. Tied to the soil for a lifetime after a youth in the cultured East, she appears bent, almost broken. The harsh Nebraskan climate has sucked her dry, turning her skin 'as yellow as a Mongolian's'. When she visits her nephew in the East — Cather in disguise — he takes her to an orchestral matinee, and all the carefully repressed memories of youth burst forth. Her cry as the concert ends is heart-breaking: 'I don't want to go, Clark, I don't want to go!' For the Nebraska which awaits Georgiana is not the splendid country of Alexandra Bergson. It is a bleak, cruel land of isolation, where music consists of Gospel hymns at the Methodist Church, where shabby turkeys vie for scraps at the kitchen door. Willa Cather had to put a great deal of distance between herself and Nebraska before she could begin to portray it with love — a distance measured in both miles and years.

None the less, in the midst of a raw country, Frances Cather found an eager mind to which she could pass on her artistic knowledge. The tales of concerts, opera, art and theatre, the high ideals she was learning from books . . . all combined to produce a longing in Willa Cather, a longing somehow bound up with that one created by stories of the Old World. In future, when she encountered the arts at first-hand, Cather's excitement would grow more 'unreasonable' than ever.

After eighteen months on the Divide, the Charles Cathers moved again; once more, the causes behind the move are not known. Growing children in need of proper schools, a wife who required medical attention — here was reason enough. It is also likely that Charles himself had never adjusted to frontier life. Both he and his wife were educated, sociable people, much better suited to the life of a town. In September 1884 another auction was held. Charles set up an office in Red Cloud where his law training could be put to some use; he wrote title abstracts, insurance policies, and made farm loans. This time only one cousin, Bess Seymore, moved with the Cathers, Mrs Boak, and Margie Anderson.

Red Cloud, Nebraska, has become one of the most well-known towns in American literature. It is the Frankfort of *One of Ours*, the Haverford of *Lucy Gayheart*, the Hanover of *O Pioneers!*, and the Sweet Water of *A Lost Lady*. It is Ántonia's Black Hawk, Thea's Moonstone, the anonymous towns of many short stories. Red Cloud was fourteen years old in 1884, and after the semi-isolation of the Divide, its two and a half thousand inhabitants must have been a welcome sight to the Cathers. The name was taken from a Sioux Indian chief who had buried his daughter on a river bluff to the south; Willa and her brothers often found arrowheads there.

The town had been founded in 1870 by the Garber brothers

who arrived on horseback to build a stockade. Silas Garber moved on to become governor of the state. He and his much younger wife Lyra returned to Red Cloud to retire, and frequently held parties at their large, spacious home. Lyra Garber was 'a flash of brightness in a grey background' to Cather, who immortalised her as Marian Forrester of *A Lost Lady* (1923).

Despite its short history, the Red Cloud of the 1880s was a thriving little community. This was due in part to its location as a division point for the Burlington railroad. Eight passenger trains a day swept through the town and, as these were the days before the dining car, Red Cloud provided meals for many a hungry traveller. Since the Burlington line had been built after the town, its tracks lay about a mile south, by the Republican River.

As in most frontier communities, a long main street ran north and south through the centre of Red Cloud. Here lay the business section, with shops and offices on either side, including the large brick-built State Bank Building. The square contained the courthouse, surrounded by cottonwood trees, which somehow managed to survive the climate. The *Nebraska State Journal* reported in 1883 that '[no] town in the state is better off in the line of churches and schools than Red Cloud' — another example of the happy accidents which pervaded the life of Willa Cather. An opera house was erected in 1885, providing her with an additional source of interest.

The Cather house was a rented affair on the corner of Third and Cedar streets, one block from the business district (see plate 4). It was small and cramped, housing nine people in one and a half storeys; privacy-loving Willa must have found it a difficult adjustment. 'All those wooden dwellings in Western towns were flimsily built . . . for people without nerves', she wrote in *Lucy Gayheart* (1935). Yet despite her moments of cynicism, Cather remembered an easy, comfortable atmosphere about the house, which she described in detail in 'Old Mrs. Harris'.

The best part of the house was the loft in the half-storey, a long room under the eaves in which the older children slept. When Willa grew older one end was partitioned to create a private room, the famous 'Rose Bower'. She clearly loved both her communal and private lives. In 'The Best Years', her last short story (completed in 1945, two years before her death), she recalls the days when she, Roscoe and Douglass shared a cub-

camaraderie in their attic room, away from prying parental eyes. But once the partition arrived, Willa guarded her tiny cubicle like a badger guarding its sett. She worked in a drugstore in return for wallpaper, decorating the room with a rose pattern. Soon it was common knowledge that no one could enter the Rose Bower without the consent of its occupant. When Willa went off to the university in Lincoln, the Bower was locked until she returned.

At last she had a place of her own where she could read as late as she liked and think her own thoughts. Thea Kronborg's room is a replica of the Rose Bower: a low ceiling, sloping on both sides; a double window to the floor; the wallpaper of tiny roses against a yellowish background; the hatbox-cum-bedtable, complete with lantern. Cather never forgot the security she felt in this room; she even placed Godfrey St Peter (*The Professor's House*, 1925) in a tiny, cluttered room under the mansard — his refuge from a changing world. Privacy and stability were just as important to Willa the child as they would become for Cather the artist.

'She seemed wholly at the mercy of accident; but to persons of her vitality and honesty, fortunate accidents will always happen.' In the preface to *The Song of the Lark*, Cather unknowingly described herself. Her life in retrospect seems riddled by such serendipity: her environment at birth; the Divide, which awoke her senses; even the little attic room, so necessary to a young artist's development. The strangest coincidence of all was Red Cloud itself. Although it looked like countless other quickly-built frontier towns, its citizens were a cosmopolitan mixture of races, talents, and intellects, in unusual proportions. She may have had a need for private space, but as an eleven-year-old 'curiosity shop', Willa Cather soon discovered that Red Cloud was full of interesting people who would teach her all they knew.

At last Willa was able to begin learning on an institutional basis. At South Ward and, later, at Red Cloud High School, she came under the eyes of some of the best educators of the day, such as Evangeline King and Mr and Mrs A.K. Goudy. Miss King was the principal of South Ward School; later, she became the superintendent of schools for Webster County. One of the first people Cather was drawn to in the town, her portrait may be found in 'The Best Years' as Evangeline Knightly. Mrs Goudy was the principal of Red Cloud High School, and when her husband was appointed state superintendent of schools the

Goudys moved to Lincoln — in the same year that Willa began her studies at the university there.

The young Willa Cather must have been a memorable pupil. She entered the school system with an extraordinary knowledge of literature — especially where her favourites such as Shakespeare were concerned — yet she could not spell correctly; she was passionate about Latin, but her grammar was in a state of disarray; in mathematics she seemed to have no aptitude whatsoever, yet the sciences fascinated her.

As is often the case, however, the most valuable and influential instructors were not found in the classroom. Red Cloud possessed men such as William Ducker, an Englishman who earned a scant living in his brother's store, but whose real interests were scientific experiments and the classics. Ducker was considered a failure by the town's merchant class, for he showed none of their zeal for profits. There were greater investments to be made: Willa read Latin and Greek with him on a regular basis. She and Ducker explored the mysteries of Virgil's *Aeneid* and the *Odes* of Anacreon. They also had many a philosophical debate, for Ducker was considered a free-thinker.

Willa received piano lessons from Professor Shindelmeisser, a German classical pianist, somewhat of a derelict, but talented all the same. It was quickly apparent that his young pupil had not the slightest interest in keyboard technique. She plagued the Professor with questions about Germany and the great composers, listening to what he played for her. Shindelmeisser eventually told Virginia Cather that she was wasting her money — Willa would never make a pianist. But Willa's mother was a woman of extraordinary insight. She insisted that the lessons be continued, for her daughter was learning far more important things than music theory. Shindelmeisser became Thea Kronborg's 'Herr Wunsch'.

An English classicist and a German musician were oddities enough for any American community, but then Red Cloud was not typical of the mould. Next door to the Cathers lived the Charles Wieners, the 'Rosens' of 'Old Mrs. Harris'. Charles was a German merchant, his wife was French, and both languages flew about the house, mixing with English in conversation. The Wieners gave Willa the run of their unusually good library. Like Vickie Templeton, she spent many afternoons there, escaping from the Nebraska heat into the cool sanctuary of books.

The library, with its soft carpets, deep velvet chairs and walls hung with engravings and watercolours, was 'the nearest thing to an art gallery and a museum' the Cathers had ever encountered. Willa often came just to lie on the carpet and gaze at the pictures. The books, however, drew her like a moth to a flame: 'There was a complete set of the Waverley Novels in German . . .many French books, and some of the German classics done into English, such as Coleridge's translation of Schiller's *Wallenstein.*'

Like Vickie, however, Cather read books only for what they could tell her and so she read everything, from trash to tragedy. The books of the Cather household provide a fair cross-section. In addition to Shakespeare, Milton, Bunyan, Dickens, Scott, Thackeray and others, there were many American writers: Emerson, Poe, and Hawthorne. There were books on the Civil War, religious books, works by Southern writers such as John Esten; there were ladies' magazines, and also volumes of poetry. Virginia Cather read the popular romantic novelists of the day — Marie Corelli, Ouida and droves of others. Doubtless Cather read them, too, for the scathing comments in her newspaper columns make it clear that she had a first-hand knowledge of them. They were not at all what she considered the highest forms of literature, yet she read them all the same, doubtless learning from her mistakes. New novels like *Madame Bovary* and *Anna Karenina* were also in evidence.

Sometime in the 1880s, Cather formed her Private Library, numbering her personal books in the fashion of the time, signing many of them 'W*m* Cather, Jr.' — an affectation she used well into her freshman year at the university. Some examples of the titles in the Private Library include the *Iliad* in translation, a three-volume edition of Homer, *The Pilgrim's Progress*, George Eliot's *The Spanish Gypsy*, *Anthony and Cleopatra*, Carlyle's *Sartor Resartus* and Alexander Winchell's *Sketches of Creation*. Added to these is her collection of childhood favourites: *The Count of Monte Cristo*, *John Halifax, Gentleman* and the medieval tales of Howard Pyle, particularly *Otto of the Silver Hand*. Robert Louis Stevenson's *Treasure Island* and Mark Twain's *Huckleberry Finn* appeared in 1883 and 1884 respectively, and both remained favourites throughout Cather's life.

Scientific knowledge was by no means omitted in a town that

housed scholars, musicians, and linguists. During adolescence Willa was firmly convinced that she wanted to study medicine. When either of the Red Cloud physicians, Dr McKeeby or Dr Damerell, called upon their patients, Willa often accompanied them, and learned to administer anaesthetics. She was once the 'anaesthesiologist' for a boy undergoing an amputation.

But life was not all scholastic learning. The young Willa was 'all over the country then', her nose 'poking into nearly everything'. She and her brothers explored the country around Red Cloud, often visiting their old friends on the Divide, or going to the river to fish and play.

The river provided an environment of water, trees, and islands: a child's paradise. Willa — always with a flair for the dramatic — created a whole world on one of the islands, which contained such places as 'The Uttermost Desert', or 'The Huge Fallen Tree'. The children sometimes camped on the island, and these happy memories evolved into two stories: 'The Treasure of Far Island' (1902), and 'The Enchanted Bluff' (1909). The latter also makes use of the children's fascination with the Spanish explorer, Coronado who, in his search for the Seven Cities of Cibola, had passed close to the river. The Old World explorer teased Cather's mind for years, and resurfaced in *The Professor's House* — Godfrey St Peter is the author of a monumental work concerned with Spanish exploration in America.

Of course there were other friends besides her brothers. Most important to Willa was the Miner family. Mrs Julia Miner, a plump Norwegian, came from Christiania (she refused to call it 'Oslo'); her father had been an oboist in Ole Bull's Royal Norwegian Orchestra. She was herself an accomplished pianist and knowledgeable about opera. Hers is the only direct portrait Cather ever admitted writing; Mrs Miner is definitely the 'Mrs. Harling' of *My Ántonia*. She had 'bright, twinkling eyes and a stubborn little chin. She was quick to anger, quick to laughter, and jolly from the depths of her soul'. Cather also remembered Mrs Miner at the piano: 'I can see her this moment: her short, square person planted firmly on the stool, her little fat hands moving quickly and neatly over the keys, her eyes fixed on the music with intelligent concentration'. Julia Miner's husband James was a Red Cloud merchant who owned a general store. The Miner children were playmates of Willa's; Mary Miner was about her own age and Carrie, the eldest, was one of the privileged few admitted to the Rose Bower — mainly because she was older and liked to discuss things. Carrie's relationship to Willa was much the same as that of 'Frances Harling' to 'Jim'.

One of Willa's favourite pastimes was play-acting; she was often asked to recite Longfellow's 'Hiawatha', a performance which included bow and arrow. She frequently wrote and directed plays for herself and the Miner children, and one of the first productions was staged in the Miner home. It was so successful that the children went on to perform *Beauty and the Beast* in the Opera House, with proceeds from the show going to the victims of the 1888 blizzard. Willa, as usual, took a male role. She played her part so convincingly that one local woman refused to believe 'that boy' had been a girl.

'Willie' Cather confused more people off the stage than on it. She was a natural rebel, strong-willed and thoroughly unconventional. In childhood she was a solemn, pretty little girl, with long, reddish-brown hair and changeable blue-grey eyes (plate 7). Adolescence reveals a changeling: gone are the lovely locks, replaced by a crew-cut and a Confederate army cap (plate 8). When Virginia Cather had been too ill after a birth to care for her daughter's hair, the wilful teenager had a barber cut it off.

In those days, Cather seems to have longed for the freedom that being male afforded. In addition to assisting the doctors on their rounds — unusual for a girl — she was given to dissecting toads and cats. She preferred 'Will' to 'Willie', dressing as much as possible in boy's clothes — shirts, ties, hats, even a cane. When asked to sign a memory book in 1888, she wrote that her 'idea of perfect happiness' was 'amputating limbs', and that a husband should possess 'lamb-like meekness'. Many of the townspeople in Red Cloud thought her eccentric.

Her own self-portrait ('Vickie' in 'Old Mrs. Harris') gives the impression that public opinion bothered her very little, if at all. We see her as an intelligent though self-absorbed adolescent, around whom life revolves; it never quite touches her.

> You couldn't tell about Vickie. She wasn't pretty yet Mrs. Rosen found her attractive. She liked her sturdy build, and the steady vitality that glowed in her rosy skin and dark blue eyes . . . A half smile nearly always played about her lips and

eyes, and it was there because she was pleased with something, not because she wanted to be agreeable.

It is as if Vickie/Willa possesses a secret that is hers and hers alone; the secret of her future, perhaps?

Whether Willa Cather was aware of her own talent remains a puzzle. For most of her childhood she denied wanting to be a writer, yet two interviews published within a week of each other show an interesting contradiction in terms: 'But I didn't want to be an author. I wanted to be a surgeon!' (*Omaha Daily News*, 29 October 1921); 'I always intended to write, and there were certain persons I studied. I seldom had much idea of the plot or the other characters, but I used my eyes and my ears' (Lincoln *Sunday Star*, 6 November 1921).

'We knew she would be *something* unusual, something special', Carrie Miner Sherwood recalled. For those who saw through the adolescent façade, Cather's quality was unmistakable. Beneath her sometimes eccentric exterior, an artist was growing up.

In 'Old Mrs. Harris', Hilary Templeton blinds himself to his daughter's coming of age. Peter Kronborg, too, is blissfully unaware of the changes and talents pulsing through Thea in *The Song of the Lark*. Both characters portray Charles Cather's vague hope that 'Daughter' would be content to live and die in the same little town, teaching awhile before she 'settled down'. That Willa Cather broke from the mould at the turn of the century is amazing enough in itself; that she did so from within a Southern family of that period is even more remarkable. She would surely have followed her art in any event, but she was certainly fortunate in having her mother on her side.

As school-days drew to an end, Virginia Cather supported Willa's plans to attend college, in spite of the financial difficulties involved. When Willa was accepted by the preparatory school at the University of Nebraska in Lincoln, Charles Cather had to borrow the money for tuition fees. But perhaps even he had caught a glimpse of his daughter's future in the commencement speech she had given at her graduation in June 1890. Willa was one of a class of three; the other two students were boys, and the group was the second to graduate from Red Cloud High School.

Cather's address was entitled 'Superstition versus Investigation'. In it, she proposed that scientific investigation was the hope of the age — an opinion she later reversed in *The Professor's House*. The makings of a writer are evident, however, and the opening line was particularly prophetic: 'All human history is a record of emigration, an exodus from barbarism to civilization'. From barbarism to civilisation; the road to the kingdom of art. At sixteen years of age, Willa Cather's exodus was just beginning.

3 Awakening

> If youth did not matter so much to itself, it would
> never have the heart to go on.
>
> *The Song of the Lark*

One hundred miles — roughly the distance the Burlington train
carried a young girl in 1890. Not very far in terms of linear
distance, in terms of personal growth and change that journey
placed light years between Willa Cather and the tiny world of
Red Cloud.

Lincoln, Nebraska, had been one of many so-called 'instant
cities' which sprang up, seemingly overnight, in the wake of the
great railroad expansion. When it became state capital in 1867, it
was little more than a dot on the prairie, but by the 1890s it
boasted a population of 30,000, a university, a library, over one
hundred churches and almost as many saloons. The city had
been laid out in a western grid pattern, not unlike that of Salt
Lake City, Utah: lettered streets ran east and west; numbered
streets, north and south.

Like the state itself, Lincoln was a mixture of nationalities and
traditions, an odd combination of Western primitivism and trans-
planted cosmopolitanism. Many of its founders had come from
the Eastern states, bringing their culture with them; in her essay
'Writer in Nebraska' Bernice Slote describes the atmosphere
created by these Eastern immigrants: 'They moved in, took out
their white kid gloves, subscribed to *Century*, shipped in oysters
frozen in blocks of ice, and tried to keep life very much as it had
been. . . .'

Although surrounded by open prairie, Cather's Lincoln was a
vibrant and lively city, with wide streets and electric trolley cars.
Visitors had their choice of five major hotels and two theatres —
the Lansing and the Funke Opera House, each with a seating
capacity of over 1,000. Situated as it was on the Burlington's
Chicago to Denver line, Lincoln played host to the many theatre
companies which had recently begun touring the country. When
both the Lansing and the Funke were in operation, around 100

27

companies a year passed through the city and there were sometimes as many as five or six different plays a week.

The University of Nebraska developed in much the same, swift fashion. Founded in 1869, its first year opened with a single college of arts, literature, and science; twenty regular and 130 preparatory students crammed themselves into the same building. By the time Willa Cather arrived, total enrolment had risen to nearly four hundred students, and four redbrick buildings graced the flat prairie campus. The largest and oldest of these, University Hall, sported a huge square bell tower; photographs from the 1890s show it dwarfing the rest of the campus, making the young trees seem like saplings in comparison. 'There was an atmosphere of endeavor, of expectancy and bright hopefulness about the young college', Cather recalled in *My Ántonia*. Like youth, it never stopped growing and changing. When Cather graduated in 1895, the student population had tripled in size.

This prairie college produced an astonishing number of high achievers. In Cather's day, there were several future leaders among the student body: four state governors; two university chancellors; two congressmen; and one US senator. Her friends included Dorothy Canfield, William Westermann, and Louise and Roscoe Pound, who became, respectively, a Pulitzer Prize-winning novelist, an authority on ancient history, a noted scholar of folklore and literary history, and the Dean of the Harvard Law School. One instructor of mathematics and military science was a young lieutenant whom the world would know later as General John J. 'Blackjack' Pershing, Commander of the American Expeditionary Forces in the First World War. William Jennings Bryan, though not directly connected with the university, opened his library to students in the evenings, and the lawyer was clearly someone Cather admired. When Bryan turned presidential candidate, she would write about his famous 'Cross of Gold' speech in the summer of 1895. Surrounded by minds such as these, Willa Cather found Lincoln to be a place of intellectual as well as cultural excitement.

Because the country schools were often inadequate, the university had organised the Latin School, a two-year preparatory course designed to help potential students meet the college's high admission requirements. Cather's education had been better than most and accordingly she was enrolled as a 'second prep' in the senior half of the course. Thus, she completed another year of training prior to her matriculation in the university proper.

According to Edith Lewis, Cather probably had no intention of becoming a writer at this time. Before entering the Latin School, Willa had written to Mrs Goudy that her chief interests were astronomy, botany, and chemistry. She was fascinated by literature *and* science, and she may well have intended to pursue both subjects — until fate decreed otherwise.

Miss Lewis's account of the first college years (no doubt largely derived from Cather herself) paints a picture of serious, studious enthusiasm. Willa rented a 'rather bleak' room in town, not far from the central business district, and set to work in earnest. This room is Jim Burden's in *My Ántonia* — actually two chambers, for Cather converted a closet into a sleeping area, and used the main space for a study. A map of Rome hung on the wall — in 1888, she had written that she wanted to visit that city above all others. She carried her own coal for heating up two flights of stairs, rose at 5 a.m. to study, often working on until late in the evenings. No grades remain from this period, but Lewis tells us that Cather stood first in a Latin class of fifty-three.

Willa Cather's powers of application are not to be doubted. Her energy was most atypical in a family that looked at life in a more leisurely fashion. During her years of study she chalked up at least eighteen semesters of English courses (including two years of Shakespeare); courses in Latin, Greek, French and German; at least one semester of journalism; and other subjects such as rhetoric, mathematics, chemistry, history (American and European) and philosophy. When set against the background of her extra-mural, and later, professional activities, this is quite an impressive record. It was this same sort of energy which led a fellow-worker at *McClure's* to opine that if Willa Cather had been a scrub-woman, she would have scrubbed much harder than other scrub-women.

But Lewis's account seems too reminiscent of those fabled five miles of arctic wasteland through which one's own grandparents trekked to school. Cather's college days were days of endeavour, but they were also happy ones and not as severe as they have sometimes been painted. For one thing, that 'bleak' room was in the home of a family friend, 'Aunt' Kate Hastings, who served some of the best meals in town. And Cather was never the 'artist in the garret' type; not during these days when the world was new and exciting. A classmate from the Latin School remembered her as a very human, impish teenager — an ally in classroom antics. In fact, the two girls 'cut up' so much that the instructor was forced to seat them on the front row. Here we have a 'Billy' Cather who wrote verse instead of listening to lectures; who side-tracked her teacher in order to escape an assignment; and who had no real enthusiasm for anything save her 'hobby', English — although she remained painstaking in other lessons.

Both portraits are accurate in their way. Miss Lewis did not meet Cather until the summer of 1903 and it was 1908 before they shared an apartment; any memories she heard from Cather were already altered by time and distance. Cather's Latin School classmate, Grace Morgan Riley, really knew Cather only in those first, enthusiastic college days.

Willa Cather was always an enigma. Letters from her classmates seem to describe a schizophrenic: on the one hand 'vivacious', 'lively', and 'courteous'; on the other 'cruel', 'cynical', and 'egotistical'. As she was admired and respected by faculty members as well as students, a good deal of detrimental opinion may be put down to simple jealousy. She was certainly outspoken, professing at one time to non-belief in God, and always spoiling for a good argument.

Her appearance did much to affect the opinions of her fellow students, for young 'William' was still dressing mannishly, though neatly, in well-cut, tailored suits. She often wore a coat over starched white shirtwaists, usually complete with ties and linked cuffs. Her full skirts were short for the era, and sometimes she added a boater-like straw hat to her outfit — all this in the age of the Gibson girl! In the Brown/Edel biography, William Westermann remembers his first encounter with this unusual figure. He and other students were sitting in a classroom, awaiting the arrival of their professor. A head appeared round the door — a head with short, shingled hair and a straw hat. A deep voice asked if this were the class for beginning Greek? When told that it was, a female body in skirts followed the head into the room, and the class dissolved in fits of laughter. Apparently unruffled, Willa Cather took her seat.

By this time she had reached her full height of around five feet three inches. Piercing blue eyes were set in a face often described as 'strong' and 'good to look at'. Her voice was low, an alto; her laugh hearty and warm. The slightest smile resulted in dimples. Whether one liked or disliked her, it appears that Willa Cather was not easily forgotten.

She studied chemistry in her freshman year, but mathematics continued to plague and exasperate her and she did not work off an incomplete in that subject until just prior to graduation. This seeming numerical inaptitude provided another reason to turn her full attention to writing. However, it was the Latin School English class which seems to have propelled her towards her life's calling.

Professor Ebenezer Hunt often set his classes to writing themes, and sometime during the winter of 1890/1 the students were given the verbose and eloquent Thomas Carlyle as their subject. Willa, already well-versed in Carlyle, attacked her paper with characteristic enthusiasm, producing an impressive example of what she later said was the kind of writing she most disliked. 'Concerning Thomas Carlyle' is indeed so flowery that it is positively rococo; none the less, it is a remarkable piece of writing for so young an essayist. Professor Hunt certainly thought so, and copied one passage on the blackboard for all to admire.

Like the lone survivor of some extinct species, the last of the mammoths, tortured and harassed beyond all endurance by the smaller, though perhaps more perfectly organized offspring of the world's maturer years, this great Titan, son of her passionate youth, a youth of volcanoes, and earthquakes, and great, unsystemized forces, rushed off into the desert to suffer alone.

What a sentence! Yet beneath its 'tortured' exterior, the author is emerging, her themes of the past, the struggle of the artist and the passion of youth already in evidence. Her first direct statement about art appears elsewhere in the essay, coupled with an important assertion on marriage.

The wife of an artist, if he continues to be an artist, must always be a secondary consideration with him; she should realize that from the outset. Art of every kind is an exacting master; more so even than Jehovah. He says only, 'Thou shalt have no other gods before me.' Art, science, and letters cry,

'Thou shalt have no other gods at all.' They accept only human sacrifices.

Here Cather has not yet let go of her interest in science, placing it in the same context as art. She has also formulated two concepts she would continue to affirm throughout her life: (1) that marriage and art are rarely compatible; and (2) that art demands total commitment and sacrifice. One seldom finds happy marriages in Cather's fiction, and her successful artists achieve their success only by the forfeit of their personal lives; they pay for their pursuit with their humanity.

Hunt, rather unethically, arranged to have the essay published without Cather's knowledge, and it appeared in the *Nebraska State Journal* on 1 March 1891. The *Hesperian*, an undergraduate newspaper, also obtained a copy and printed it on the same date. At the age of seventeen, Willa Cather was a published writer — a situation which probably surprised her more than anyone else. Seeing her name in print acted like a catalyst; from that point on, there was no turning back, and science fell by the wayside. Desire had been brought to the fore, made conscious. She had no idea where a writing life would lead her, or even of the type of thing she wished to write — but she was determined to find out. Like Thea Kronborg, the young Willa Cather was hurtling headlong towards her future self: a translator of life, a channel of art, a writer!

The *Journal* printed another essay in two parts during November 1891. 'Shakespeare and Hamlet' defends the Bard and his Danish prince against those analysts who read meaning into every detail, decrying the natural form and emotion of the play. Shakespeare never intended *Hamlet* as a puzzle, Cather declared; if he wrote himself into the play, then he did so unconsciously: 'It may be his feeling and individuality were wrought up intensely, and crept into the play which he happened to be writing'.

Cather herself wrote this way, much more so than she either realised or admitted. The secret of Shakespeare's genius, she said, lay in 'supreme love', not supreme intellect; it was a love not only for the ideal, but also for reality, 'which is but a form of the ideal after all'. This argument for emotion is slightly distorted, taken to that romantic extreme which is so attractive to young artists. It is evident, however, that even at this early age Willa Cather had been seriously pondering the pursuit of art for some time. Emotion was superior to intellect, a higher plane reached only through the door of suffering and isolation. 'If an artist does any good work he must do it alone', she wrote. 'He who walks with the crowd is drawn to its level.'

In actual fact, Cather was not as aloof in those days as she liked to believe — romantics seldom are. Her nature was such that it demanded human contact; if she was selective in her friends, she certainly had no lack of them — older ones like the Goudys and solid new ones of all ages: the Gere, Canfield and Westermann families; the Pounds (brother and sisters); and Dr Julius Tyndale.

James Canfield was chancellor of the University of Nebraska from 1891–6, and his daughter, Dorothy, was one of Willa's closest friends despite the difference in their ages (Dorothy was six years Willa's junior). It seems inevitable that two future novelists should find each other, and they even collaborated on a story for the *Sombrero*, the college yearbook. Dorothy supplied the plot, Willa wrote it, and 'The Fear the Walks by Noonday' won them a $10 prize in 1894.

The Gere family adopted Willa as one of their own. She and Mariel Gere were early comrades, and in time Mariel's sisters, Frances and Ellen, also became her friends. Mariel's father, Charles H. Gere, was the editor of the *Journal*, her future employer. Mrs Gere saw through Willa's boyish façade. 'She's not at all masculine', she told her daughter, and soon 'Billy' found herself wearing feminine blouses and letting her hair grow.

Cather seems always to have been drawn to German friends, from the Lambrechts on the Divide to the Seibels in Pittsburg. The Louis Westermanns were a cultured family who lived in a fine house on S Street, near the university. Mr Westermann owned Lincoln's *Evening News*, and his wife, Emma, appears to have fascinated the girl from the prairies. Together with their six sons, the Westermanns became the 'Erlichs' of *One of Ours*. Like Claude, Willa found their way of life irresistible and the rendering of Claude's visits to the Erlichs is drawn from many a Sunday she spent in the Westermann household.

Emma Westermann's brother, Dr Julius Tyndale, formed an attachment to the girl from Red Cloud, a relationship which evidently caused a certain amount of gossip among the local busybodies. Tyndale was the 'Toby Rex' of the *Evening News*, a physician who wrote dramatic criticism as a sideline. At fifty, he was still a bachelor, active, and an iconoclast; he took a lively interest in Cather, escorted her to concerts and was responsible for sending her to Chicago for an opera week in 1895.

Cather was also seen in the company of Charles Moore, the son of Charles Cather's business associate, R.E. Moore. Charles is thought to have given Willa the golden snake ring she wore for the rest of her life; if there had been any romantic involvement, however, it was probably Willa who ended it. She had no time for such things with her career to consider.

Friends could be lost as well as gained. Cather had been close to all the Pounds — Roscoe, Louise, and Olivia. During her freshman year, she and Louise were associate editors of a short-lived literary magazine called *The Lasso*. Later, however, when she satirised Roscoe in one of ther infamous *Hesperian* 'roasts', the entire Pound clan turned its collective back on her.

More than once her brash, outspoken opinions brought Cather into head-on collisions with instructors — and particularly with Professor Lucius Sherman, head of the English Department. Sherman was the author of books bearing titles such as *Elements of Literature and Composition* and *Analytics of Literature*, in which he sought to subject linguistics and literature to his own bizarre scientific method. Not all of his ideas were bad, but his analysis drove Willa Cather to distraction. He often studied a story or poem by using word counts, sentence lengths and diagrams, trying to develop a universal formula for all branches of literature. Sherman was particularly fond of the minuscule. Typical of one examination was the question: 'And what did the noble matron Volumnia say then?' Willa Cather, ready to explode, replied: 'The noble matron Volumnia then said, "Bow-wow"'. So strong was the memory of her distaste for Sherman that cutting references to advocates of analysis appear time and again throughout her fiction. Sherman became another victim of *Hesperian* satire, and when Willa began writing for the *Journal* she frequently waged war with him in her reviews; the professor wrote a book column for the rival *Evening News*.

There was reason for her exasperation. Cather had only to compare Sherman with another instructor, Herbert Bates, to see how she had been abused intellectually. Bates had come to

Lincoln from New England in 1891 and, in spite of his biting sarcasm, he became a popular and influential teacher of English. He did much to encourage the young writer, and helped her with her stories. Himself a capable poet and short-story writer, Bates appears to be the 'Gaston Cleric' of *My Ántonia*. Judging from that portrait, Willa Cather may have had something of a student crush on her teacher.

But Bates was not the main reason that Sherman infuriated her. When she entered Sherman's class, Cather had already had one signed piece of work in the *Journal*. 'Shakespeare and Hamlet' seems to have been a direct reaction to Sherman's ideas, for it appeared less than two months after she entered his junior Shakespeare class. But perhaps the greatest re-enforcement of her artistic convictions came when *The Mahogany Tree* in Boston accepted her short story 'Peter', and published it in the issue of 21 May 1892. First recognition in a magazine is a heady experience for any writer; how much more so when the writer is eighteen. It was to be nearly three years before Cather again published her fiction outside the university papers. Doubtless, however, this experience only reinforced the beliefs and concepts already at work in her mind, and probably made her all the more difficult to teach.

'Peter' tells the story of Peter Sadeleck, an old Bohemian immigrant so ill-suited to life on the plains that he ends it all by shooting himself. Derived from the real-life tragedy of Francis Sadilek, Cather published revised versions of the story at least twice more before incorporating it into *My Ántonia*. Though not especially fine, the story is nevertheless a very readable first effort, and reveals a good deal about its author's state of mind and the directions she would take.

In the first version, Peter is a figure to be pitied in one sense, but he is also rather despicable. A former orchestral violinist, he hates the strange new land, has given up all hope, and refuses familial responsibility. Antone, his son, has worked and kept the Sadelecks alive, but in the process has become a slave-driver. When Antone decides to sell his father's violin — Peter's only link with the Old World and thus, with art — Peter takes his last, definitive action:

He took Antone's shotgun down from its peg, and loaded it by the moonlight which streamed in through the door. He sat down on the dirt floor, and leaned back against the dirt wall. . . . Near him he heard the regular breathing of the horses in the dark. . . . He held his fiddle under his chin a moment, where it had lain so often, then put it across his knees and broke it through the middle. He pulled off his old boot, held the gun between his knees with the muzzle against his forehead, and pressed the trigger with his toe.

The violin's bow, however, remains unbroken, and Antone coolly takes it away to sell. There are many religious references in the story which suggest that Peter was willing to risk eternal damnation for commiting suicide, rather than give up his art. Likewise, Willa Cather would write to Mariel Gere from Pittsburgh that she was willing to follow her art to a much more hellish place than that city if necessary.

The *Hesperian* printed 'Peter' in November. A poem, 'Shakespeare/A Freshman Theme', had appeared in June — her first published poetry. Three signed stories followed: 'Lou, the Prophet' (October 1892), 'A Tale of the White Pyramid' (December 1892) and 'A Son of the Celestial' (January 1893). The latter two stories are experiments in the mysterious, while in 'Lou', one finds a forerunner of Crazy Ivor in *O Pioneers!*

The next story appeared unsigned, but it clearly belongs to Willa Cather. 'The Elopement of Allen Poole' (April 1893) shows Cather's first use of Virginia as a setting. It was left unsigned most probably to avoid possible repercussions. Statements such as: 'It takes a man of the South to do nothing properly' would not have been particularly welcome in Cather's family, had they caught sight of them with Willa's name attached. She returned to the Midwest in the next (signed) story, 'The Clemency of the Court' (October 1893), a horrific account of an ill-fated Russian immigrant. Two poems and a translation of Horace also appeared in the *Hesperian* (1892–3).

In terms of real literary worth, not much can be gained by delving into every story or poem that Cather produced in these early years. The author, indeed, bitterly resented any reference to them, preferring to deny their existence. Yet they are valuable as artist's sketches, for they show quite clearly the writer's development. Ideas and contrasts she later used continuously are already present: age and youth; old values and new; suicides; madness;

the 'European' versus the 'American'. The first treatment of Nebraska, however, portrays a harsh, cruel land — suggesting that Cather's initial childhood feelings of resentment took longer to dissolve than she was ever to admit.

At some point during 1892, Willa Cather wrote to Mrs Goudy admitting that she could never be a scholar. By this time, she had become an associate editor of the *Hesperian*, writing editorials, satire, and criticism in addition to her poems and stories, and earning the reputation which led to her selection as managing editor the following year.

The *Hesperian* was the oldest university newspaper, a joint effort of the literary societies which formed a central part of student social life. The societies — Palladian, Delian, and Union — met regularly to hold debates, dramatisations, orations, and sometimes musical programmes. Cather joined the Union, in which she held several offices.

Most of her outside activities reflected her artistic interests. In addition to belonging to the Union, she was a member of the Lewis Carroll Society. She also gained a reputation as an actress of some talent, after appearing in at least two productions of the University Dramatic Society. And all the while she was writing.

The year 1893 brought about many changes in Cather's student life, not the least of which was a journalism course conducted by William Owen Jones, the managing editor of the *Journal*, who became a lifelong friend. The course did not begin until the spring of 1894, but in the autumn of 1893 Jones organised a journalism club, for which students received English credits. Cather may have taken part in this club, although her name does not appear in connection with it. At any rate, she began to write for the *Journal* during this time.

Lincoln possessed five major newspapers during this period, but the *Journal* was the largest and most substantial of the lot. Its Sunday arts and features section showed remarkable flair, at times publishing poems by Rudyard Kipling, a translation of a Turgenev story, a new novel by Robert Louis Stevenson. There were also regular reviews of plays, concerts and other entertainment. Cather's association with the paper raised its criticism to an even higher standard — so high, in fact, that in 1895 the Des Moines *Record* could comment: 'The best theatrical critics of the west are said to be connected with the Lincoln, Neb., press.' The two top critics were Cather and her friend, 'Toby Rex'.

Why the move to journalism? Cather had just begun to search for her art; she had only just started experimenting with style and characterisation. The answer must lie, at least in part, in necessity.

The year 1893 was the first of Nebraska's 'panic years' — two blistering, brutal summers that turned Nebraska into a dust-bowl. Unremitting drought caused large-scale crop failures; more than a hundred banks closed throughout the state. The freezing winter of 1894/5 served only to add death and disease, and relief aid poured in from all over the country.

Back home in Red Cloud, Charles Cather barely avoided bankruptcy. His own land investments were heavily mortgaged and the farmers who owed him money either couldn't or wouldn't pay. Sixteen-year-old Roscoe took a teaching post in the county school, but even so hard times had arrived for Willa Cather's family. She was not destitute but she needed to become as self-sufficient as possible. Quite simply, she could not afford to refuse the dollar a column the *Journal* offered — nor is it likely that she wanted to. What writer in her twentieth year could resist such a challenge? During the next two-and-a-half years, Cather was to produce over 300 separate pieces, many of essay length: they included reviews of drama, concerts, and art exhibitions, as well as some feature stories and profiles.

She began on 5 November 1893, with an unsigned Sunday column. 'One Way of Putting It' consisted of brief human interest pieces on various topics: a Salvation Army meeting; a dance-hall pianist; a father's first encounter with his child. Her first signed review appeared in December. These columns and reviews would merge and expand under many headings, until they were at last consolidated as 'The Passing Show' in July 1895.

Cather always drew a definite line between her journalism and her art and journalism paid the rent. It also allowed her to work off the 'purple flurry' of her early writing, that same adjective-ridden style of the Carlyle essay. Charles Gere and Will Owen Jones gave her almost complete freedom, and she channelled all her youthful energy into copy, instead of stories, saying exactly what she thought. Concerning a Salvation Army meeting, the subject, 'being saved': 'Let us give the church as well as the devil its dues. By what is a man ever saved other than by enthusiasm? . . .A genius is just another way of defining a great enthusiast' (5 November 1893). Note the characteristic linking of religion and art/genius, and of that same genius with enthusiasm. In *The Song of the Lark*, Harsanyi tells a reporter that Thea's secret is that of every artist: 'passion'.

Although her reviews encompassed all aspects of creative work, the theatre had pride of place in her work. Cather had always been stage-struck, even in the days when 'the stage' meant provincial players in the Red Cloud Opera House. The talent passing through turn-of-the-century Lincoln varied enormously; vaudeville acts such as Hermann the Magician played on the stage that Modjeska had graced the week before. Dramatic productions ran the gamut from *Beau Brummell* to Shakespeare — and there were both excellent and ludicrous interpretations of the Bard.

None the less, Willa Cather witnessed performances by many famous names of the day: Richard Mansfield, Clara Morris, the Kendals, Joe Jefferson, Julia Marlowe and the 'great Pole', Helena Modjeska. When the stars didn't come to Lincoln, Cather, when possible, went to them — she saw her beloved Bernhardt in Omaha, and sampled the operatic talents of Melba in Chicago.

'Nothing can be more natural than nature, more lifelike than life.' Cather wrote this of Clara Morris in *Camille*, which she saw in 1893. Her preferences in actors and actresses largely reflected her literary tastes; she sought honesty and truth in acting just as she did in writing.

After completing a special Charter Day issue of the *Hesperian* in February 1894, Cather was able to launch full-force into her review work. She led a Jekyll and Hyde existence — student by day, critic by night; often she worked into the small hours at the *Journal* office after a performance, to set down her impressions before they grew cold in her veins. During 1894 alone she reviewed at least fifty performances, hammering out her principles as she did so: mediocrity is the worst possible situation; art carries its own reason for being; genius means 'relentless labor and passionate excitement from the hour one is born until the hour one dies'.

Gradually, Cather worked her way into other areas — music, painting, literature. Her reviews were often stimulated by news reports; 1894, for example, was a year of great change in the literary world. Oscar Wilde was on trial in England; the French Academy had refused to admit Emile Zola yet again. There were also deaths: Oliver Wendell Holmes in October; Willa's dear Robert Louis Stevenson and Christina Rossetti in December. Rossetti's 'Goblin Market' Cather considered the 'one perfect poem', and from it she derived the epigraph for her first collection of short stories, *The Troll Garden* (1905). George du Maurier's *Trilby* was shocking the world — at least the American one; typically, Cather loved it ('The trouble is that she is not bad enough').

What was to be a life-long allegiance to France began to emerge. 'George Meredith, Thomas Hardy, and Henry James excepted', she wrote, 'the great living novelists are Frenchmen.' Just as she admired French writers of the past — Hugo, Sand, Balzac — her loyalties transferred to Zola, Daudet, and Loti. Oddly enough, Flaubert is rarely mentioned.

From Russia, Cather admired Tolstoy, placing him beside Turgenev and Dostoevsky. From England she chose Austen and Thackeray, George Eliot and Henry Fielding. Among her favourite contemporary poets were Verlaine, Swinburne and Kipling, who would be followed by Housman and Yeats. There were few Americans, either poets or novelists, although she grudgingly admired Whitman (from whom she took the title for *O Pioneers!*). Among writers of the past, she adored Poe and Hawthorne. And there was always Henry James, though one could hardly classify him as being typically American. Looking back over her reviews, it is apparent that Cather's critical perception was surprisingly accurate.

From the many millions of words that she read as well as wrote, another universal premise evolved: 'The talent for writing is largely the talent for living, and is utterly independent of knowledge. . . . There is only one way to see the world truly, and that is to see it in a human way. . . . The ultimate truths are never seen through the reason, but through the imagination . . .' (*Journal*, 28 October 1894).

Perfect art — the highest art; ultimate, human truth. But what about other forms of art, those at the so-called lower planes? Cather was very fair. She never judged an artist harshly as long as he stayed within the boundaries of his own limitations (a comedian of the day was described as an artist 'in his sphere').

Those who stepped out of bounds, however, felt the swift sting of the *Journal* critic's pen. When Lillian Lewis, a third-rate actress in a suburban company, aspired to play Shakespeare, Cather left no holds barred, and obviously relished the chance to use her nimble wit: '. . . . a barge drew up and from it descended a large, limp, lachrymose 'Kleo-paw-tra', with an Iowa accent, a St. Louis air and the robust physique of a West England farmer's wife. . . . She draped and heaved her ample form about . . . she fainted . . . it was a regular landslide' (*Journal*, 23 October 1895). At the time Cather was writing for both the *Journal* and another paper, the *Lincoln Courier*, in which she could not resist a final jab: 'I shall see her in my dreams, that coy, kittenish matron, bunched up on a moth-eaten tiger stroking Mark Antony's double chin . . . I have seen waiters in restaurants who were ten times more queenly' (*Courier*, 26 October 1895).

Poor Lillian Lewis! Not for nothing did Will Owen Jones christen his fiery critic 'that meat-ax young girl'. It was a pity that Cather never allowed her sense of humour a freer rein in her fiction, for she was a skilled satirist. But then, satire was not the highest form of art.

Her reactions to women of talent during this period are strongly and surprisingly negative: 'Women can paint pictures and write novels, but never while the world stands will a woman mould a great statue or write a great play . . .' (*Journal*, 5 April 1894); 'I have not much faith in women in fiction. They have a sort of sex consciousness that is abominable. They are so few, the ones who really did anything worth while . . .' (*Courier*, 23 November 1895). She favoured the Georges (Sand and Eliot) 'who were anything but women'; also the Brontës and Jane Austen.

In 1896 she was still questioning: 'Has any woman ever really had the art instinct, the art necessity? . . . But no, there was Sappho and the two great Georges. . .' (*Journal*, 3 May 1896). Cather's reviews suggest that women may be great interpreters, hence, actresses, but that they are seldom successful as creators. This was all before she met Sarah Orne Jewett.

The months passed and all the time Cather was turning out copy for a living, passing her exams largely, as Lewis says, 'by inspiration'. She had gained a reputation throughout the West as the '*Journal* critic', a notorious roaster (not altogether true), and an extremely competent, gifted journalist — a long way indeed from those first, awkward vignettes. In addition to her professional work, Cather had both written for and edited the *Hesperian* and the *Sombrero*, and she had sampled the world of teaching. During the summer of 1894, Will Owen Jones arranged for her to teach a journalism course at the Annual Nebraska Chautauqua Assembly — an event she also covered for the *Evening News*. Her future seems to have been predetermined, for all of these experiences were soon to play a part in her career.

In February 1895 a young reporter arrived in Lincoln, sent by the Bachellor-Johnson Syndicate to report on the effects of the drought. This was Stephen Crane, whose *Red Badge of Courage* had been serialised in the *Journal*. Since Crane used the *Journal* office as a base, it is probable that Cather met him. However, her resulting article about him is most certainly fiction, and serves as another example of the continuous interplay between her experience and her imagination.

Mary L. Jones, a university librarian, accompanied Cather to Chicago during the week of 10 March, for the Metropolitan Opera season. They heard performances of works by Verdi and Meyerbeer; the great Australian soprano, Nellie Melba, was there, singing in Gounod's *Romeo and Juliet*. It was a wonderful and exhilarating experience for Willa Cather; thus Chicago's musical world figures heavily in *The Song of the Lark* and *Lucy Gayheart*.

She graduated from the university in June, but did not lie fallow for long. In August, Sarah Butler Harris, another Lincoln newspaperwoman, invited Cather to work for the *Courier* as associate editor. She remained with the *Courier* until the end of November, when, for some unknown reason, she took 'The Passing Show' back to the *Journal*.

In between her journalistic jaunts, she found time to write 'On the Divide', which the *Overland Monthly* published in January, 1896 — her first publication in a national magazine.

The year had certainly been productive, but it was, all the same, a frustrating one for Willa Cather. She had not yet begun a full-time career, or found her place in the creative world, and home life was beginning to suffocate her (one letter she wrote from Red Cloud during this time was even date-lined 'Siberia'). In the spring of 1896 she applied for a teaching position at the university in Lincoln, but her application was turned down: Lucius Sherman was still head of the English Department, and the old feud had never really been laid to rest. 'A Night at Greenway Court' appeared in the June issue of the *Nebraska Literary Magazine*, but that seemed a small consolation. There had been so many prophecies of greatness; everyone was waiting for her to prove herself . . . and she seemed to be getting nowhere.

Then came the 'mystery meeting' at the Gere's in Lincoln. Cather is thought by some biographers to have met a Mr Axtell in the Gere houschold (scholars do not agree on his name, which I have seen listed as both 'Charles' and 'James'). A letter to Mariel Gere, however, indicates that she had not met Mr Axtell before. Whether via the Geres or through connections with a college friend, George Gerwig, Axtell, a Pennsylvania business-man, offered Cather a position in the editorial office of the new *Home Monthly* magazine, a publication he hoped would rival the prestigious *Ladies' Home Journal*.

She accepted at once. It was not the kind of writing she liked, but this was a chance to get out in the world, a ticket to the East and to another life. By the end of June 1896 Willa Cather was on her way to Pittsburgh.

4 Interlude

One cannot divine nor forecast the conditions that
will make happiness; one only stumbles upon them
by chance in a lucky hour at the world's end
somewhere . . .

Nebraska State Journal, 10 September 1902

Culture, as everyone knew, resided in the East, and Cather was
elated to be on her way there at last. Indeed, as the train swept
past Chicago and the landscape changed into hills, streams, and
woodlands she was overjoyed; she felt as if she were going home.
At the end of that journey, however, lay what seemed to be the
most incongruous of artistic environments.

The Pittsburgh of the 1890's was a massive city of over a quarter
of a million people, south-western Pennsylvania's manufacturing
metropolis, which sprawled at the juncture of the Allegheny and
Monongahela rivers. Here the industrial giants reigned: Heinz,
Mellon and Westinghouse among others. Andrew Carnegie and
Henry C. Frick had already established the city as the centre of
America's mighty iron and steel industry. Glassworks, mines,
factories and steel mills flourished, their chimneys fouling the air,
their immigrant workforce filling the ghettos. To Cather, fresh
from the open prairie, these were ugly surroundings. Pittsburgh
was a 'City of Dreadful Dirt', where money was God; life, a
wealth-war; and men measured success in terms of decimal
points. To make matters worse, the social strata was dominated
by stern, inflexible Presbyterians, who (she felt) disapproved of
all forms of emotion and enjoyment — particularly enjoyment of
an aesthetic nature.

But these dour church-goers and money-mad tycoons were the
very men whose wealth supported the artistic underworld; they
were the Philistines who fostered Bohemia, providing more cultural opportunities than Cather's eyes had ever seen. For a start,
Pittsburgh offered no fewer that seven major theatres. The great
Carnegie Institute had been established in 1895, endowing the
populus with a natural history museum, an art museum, a library,

and the Carnegie Music Hall — all testimony to Andrew Carnegie's belief in his own 'Gospel of Wealth'. Cather may have lambasted the steel town and its patrons in her Lincoln columns, but the artistic experiences Pittsburgh afforded were certainly rich enough to keep her culturally occupied for the next ten years.

She arrived during the first week of July 1896 and was greeted by Mr Axtell, who took her to his family home. There she would stay until suitable accommodation could be found. The Axtells were pleasant, well-meaning people but they epitomised Pittsburgh Presbyterianism; Cather found their hospitablity suffocatingly formal. It was with great relief that she moved to a boarding-house in the East Liberty section of the city, not far from the offices of the *Home Monthly*. Mid-July found her fully entrenched in the new job, determined to make a go of it and to learn all she could in the process.

The *Home Monthly*, as James Woodress observed, 'was not much of a magazine'. 'Domestic, didactic, and highly moral' were the words Edith Lewis chose, and Cather herself described its contents as trashy. It had originally been launched in 1894 as the *Ladies' Journal*, a hopeful, cheaper imitation of Curtis and Bok's wildly successful *Ladies' Home Journal*. Axtell, Orr and Company assumed ownership in June 1896, and the first revamped edition appeared in August. An editorial from that issue defined the magazine's target audience and outlined its aims: *Home Monthly* intended to reach the half-million firesides within a hundred-mile radius of Pittsburgh, covering every aspect of 'home needs', the overall purpose being 'to entertain, to elevate, to educate'. Willa Cather had already formed her opinions of such magazines, and she had no illusions as to the type of material the publishers of *Home Monthly* required — 'Care of Children's First Teeth', 'The Origin of Thanksgiving', and 'Nursing as a Profession for Women', were typical articles. But she was willing to work in a professional way; the pay was good ($100 a month) and the job gave her publishing experience, as well as a vantage-point from which to move on to other and better things.

Axtell hired her as an editorial assistant. Shortly after she arrived, however, he took his family off on vacation and Cather was left alone to bring out the August issue, serving as editor in everything but name. There were not enough articles in reserve, so she wrote over half the first issue herself. The printers were inexperienced; she supervised and coached them. One night she even found herself laying out page formes, no doubt blessing her *Hesperian* and *Sombrero* experience in the process. Then there were all the regular editorial duties — commissioning articles, reading manuscripts, and so on — which she performed with the help of one secretary, who (fortunately) was an accurate speller. The work was certainly a challenge, if nothing else, and the magazine provided a vehicle for her own work.

In addition to the usual articles and editorials, Cather placed six poems, nine stories, and a translation of a Heine poem, 'The Three Holy Kings', in the *Home Monthly*; some of these were signed, some were pseudonymous, after the fashion of the day. Because of the limitations imposed by the general tone and format of the magazine, most of these stories are not terribly important in terms of her literary development. One, however, does stand out. 'Tommy, the Unsentimental' (August 1896) shows the author's first positive, even sympathetic treatment of Nebraska; it seems that the combined shock of distance and an unlovely environment was required before Cather could begin to consider the good elements of Midwestern life. 'Tommy' also provides an interesting little self-portrait. The main character, a young woman who bears a masculine nickname, lives in the prairie town of Southdown, an early projection of Red Cloud. Tommy has been to school in the East, where she didn't quite fit in — perhaps indicating Willa Cather's initial response to her own move east. She is comfortable in the society of older men, plays billiards, mixes cocktails — even daring to take one herself now and again. Although fond of 'Jay', whom she heroically saves from a bank failure, Tommy none the less pairs him up with an Eastern girl better suited to his life style, then returns to the business of making her way in the world. East and West are contrasted throughout, no doubt reflecting the comparisons in the forefront of the writer's mind at the time.

Although the initial adjustment had been a strenuous one, it wasn't long before Willa Cather had mastered the routine at the *Home Monthly*, and soon she was casting about for more interesting work. During the autumn of 1896, she took a position as part-time drama critic for the *Daily Leader*, a prestigious Pittsburgh newspaper, and in December of the same year 'The Passing Show' appeared once again in the Lincoln *Journal*. A part of her earnings was sent back to the family in Red Cloud, for times were still hard there, and would be for some time. What with one thing and another, her first weeks in Pittsburgh were so busy that her recreation was limited to racing the electric street-cars on the bicycle she pedalled to and from work.

Ironically, as Cather's workload increased, so did her social life, expanding with a sudden rush that left the young woman amazed and pleasantly bewildered. No chance of being a private person now: here was a new life for a new Willa Cather who seemingly bore no resemblance to the 'William' of college days. Her free hours were filled with Press Club picnics and weekend trips to the mountains. Once she joined a riverboat party hosted by George Gerwig — the guests sailed up and down the Ohio, dining by candlelight as a band serenaded them with soft music. Mrs Gerwig took her to a tea presented by the city's federated women's club, where the subject for discussion happened to be Thomas Carlyle. When the members politely requested a few words from the newcomer, Willa Cather rose and launched into her Latin School essay, reciting with such verve that her audience was completely bowled over.

She was soon to regret this success. Shortly afterwards, she wrote, various clubs were pestering her day and night, driving her to the point of near-distraction. Such women's organisations were later to receive the full blast of Cather's prose, yet she admitted to belonging to at least six of them herself during the Pittsburgh years — a contradiction linked, perhaps, to a secret desire for acceptance in this new society. She would never be a total convert to the city, however, and somehow found the time to escape its grime on a bicycle trip through the Shenandoah Valley in October, where presumably she visited her old home territory around Back Creek.

Cather's position on the *Home Monthly* lasted for just one year. In July 1897 Axtell sold his interests in the magazine to T.E. Orr, and Willa, on vacation in Red Cloud, resigned at the same time, for reasons that remain unknown — although she continued to contribute articles to the magazine until 1899. It is clear from her letters that she planned to return to Pittsburgh and work as a newspaperwoman, but in the meantime she was quite happy to be writing for herself.

Opportunity to return to the East was swift in coming. On 31

August, she received a wire from the *Leader* office, offering her a job as assistant editor on the telegraph desk. By September she was back in Pittsburgh mastering yet another set of duties, writing headlines and editing the copy which came in over the wire. She was paid just $75 a month for the position, but the hours were preferable to those of the *Home Monthly*: 8 a.m. to 3 p.m. on weekdays, and until midnight on Saturdays. The *Leader* also paid extra for any dramatic criticism she submitted. Although not quite as outspoken as before, the Nebraskan's argumentative nature was still very prevalent, a characteristic no doubt considered masculine for the times. Soon the telegraph editor, Edwin P. Couse, was calling her by the old nickname of 'Bill'.

Yet the Willa Cather who returned to Pittsburgh in 1897 seems to have been much more open to friendships of all kinds, including those of eligible young men: no less than five were waiting to meet her when she stepped off the train. Certainly men — women too, for that matter — interested her if they themselves were interesting. Serious relationship were another matter entirely. We know that Cather received at least two proposals of marriage, one of which she apparently considered seriously. Both times, however, the answer was 'No'. Cather evidently had no desire for a permanent, intimate heterosexual relationship, or if she did it was consciously denied. Betrothed to art, her earliest beliefs about marriage hadn't altered. Freedom, independence . . . these were the necessities. A husband would have been an enemy to her creativity and to herself, just like the Oswald of *My Mortal Enemy*.

Woodress suggests that Cather's deepest male loves were her father and her brothers, Roscoe and Douglass, and Cather's own comments seem to support this opinion. In a review centering on George Eliot's *The Mill on the Floss*, she lavishly praises the brother/sister bond that exists between Tom and Maggie Tulliver — in her view, the supreme portrait of the strongest, most satisfying relationship of human life. Even so, the point should be made that the bond in question arises from *childhood*. Both in the review and in remembrances of her brothers, Cather speaks most often of that special cub-love which occurs before individuals grow up and apart, often becoming strangers, as Thea Kronborg sadly discovers. At twenty-four, the past had already become a haven for the young Willa Cather.

But there was still the urgent need for love in the present, a circle of friends for family, security and shared happiness. Cather kept up with her old friends through frequent correspondence; happily, Dorothy Canfield paid several visits on her way to and from Ohio State University. And the intimate circle slowly widened, admitting new lives to be cherished, such as George and Helen Seibel, a young couple of German extraction. George himself was a writer; he and Willa met in the offices of the *Home Monthly* when he came there to discuss an article on Richard Wagner. Seibel was rather taken aback by the editor, who, he thought, 'looked about 18', but soon Cather was visiting the Seibel house twice a week, to read French and occasional German, and to play with the baby, Erna. The Seibels and Cather shared an admiration of many of the same authors — the only serious disagreement concerned Henry James, whom George Seibel disliked. In an article in the *New Colophon*, he recalls many evenings spent reading Daudet, de Musset, Hugo, Loti, Anatole France, and Gautier. Flaubert was another common passion; Willa particularly liked *Salammbô*. It proved a warm and satisfactory friendship, with familial overtones. Byrne suggests that the Engelhardt home of 'Double Birthday' (1929) is based upon the Seibel residence.

May Willard, head of the children's department at the Carnegie Library, became another life-long friend, as did Lawrence and Ethel Litchfield. Dr Litchfield was a prominent physician. His wife — perhaps the 'Caroline Noble' of 'The Garden Lodge' (1905) — had been a concert pianist, and gave many parties for visiting musicians, to which Willa was frequently invited. In Margaret Hall Slack she found another musical friend; Mrs Slack held gatherings in her elegant suburban home in Edgeworth, and her house and music room became incorporated into the setting of 'Uncle Valentine' (1925).

It may well have been at the Slack home that Willa Cather met Ethelbert Nevin, the first true artist friend of her life. Nevin, a gifted pianist and composer, had spent most of his life in Europe and Africa; some time during 1898 he returned to his boyhood home of Vineacre, next door to the Slacks. Cather, familiar with his music since Red Cloud days, reviewed his concerts in her columns. However they met, the two quickly became close friends. She often spent Sundays at Vineacre to talk with the composer and to hear him play. Nevin's 'La Lune Blanche' was dedicated to Cather, and most critics agree that it is he who lies behind the main character of 'Uncle Valentine', and is the 'Adriance Hilgard' of 'A Death in the Desert' (1903).

It is not surprising that Cather was entranced by Nevin. His music was romantic and emotional; moreover, he possessed 'the two finest thing the sun shines upon' — youth and art. Her association with him greatly increased her knowledge of music, a knowledge repeatedly woven into her works. Nevin's sudden death at the comparatively young age of thirty-eight only immortalised him in her eyes, and his spirit is recalled in three memorial poems: 'Sleep, Minstrel, Sleep' (1903); 'Arcadian Winter' (1902); and 'Song' (1903). Poe, Keats, Stevenson . . . those whom the gods favour die young. Age seems to have terrified Cather, perhaps due to memories of Grandmother Boak's latter days; youth became an obsessional subject, appearing over and over again throughout her writing.

If youth was one obsession, however, creative culture proved to be another, even stronger one. Despite its pollution and religious restrictions, a myriad of artists passed through turn-of-the-century Pittsburgh and provided the young reviewer with a wealth of material for 'The Passing Show'. Between the telegraph desk, her articles and reviews and her social life, there was too little time for fiction; most of the stories produced between 1896 and 1900 had been tailor-made for the *Home Monthly*. A fallow period is, none the less, necessary at times. Cather was an artist who needed to experience life intensely over a long period before she could recreate it with power. While these were frustrating years in terms of creative output, they were also years of absorption, both conscious and unconscious — especially within the intersecting worlds of music and theatre which she was discovering now as never before.

She could not get enough of the theatre. 'I saw Miss Nethersole four times as Carmen', she wrote in her columns. 'I have seen Minnie Madern Fiske as Tess of the D'Urbervilles four times this week.' Seibel recalls her watching Bernhardt perform on four consecutive nights in 1901. This was no passing fancy; Cather was a woman in her late twenties, well past the age when such extremes could be put down to crushes. There are hints of the obsession of 'Paul's Case' (1905) — but unlike Paul, Cather's fascination stemmed from the human beings behind the art of drama. She was an entity, Seibel said, 'with eyes in every pore'; 'a prospector in the deep and quiet lodes of the soul'.

She was also naturally drawn to music — listening to it with her heart and her emotions, not with her intellect. Music, as Edith Lewis recalls, was for Willa Cather 'an emotional experience that had a potent influence on her imaginative process', and these were emotional and imaginative times indeed. Dvořák's Symphony in E minor — the 'New World' Symphony — was being performed all over the United States. From the moment she first heard it in 1894, Cather readily identified with this music of a youthful nation; so, too, does Thea Kronborg. Walter Damrosch brought the operas of Wagner to America — *Lohengrin* and *Die Walküre* figure heavily in *The Song of the Lark*.

But music, even of this calibre, was, for Cather, subordinate to the beings who brought it to life: Schumann-Heink, Calvé, Eames, Nordica, Melba . . . she heard them all, time and again. Actresses, especially prima donnas, intrigued her, perhaps because they, more than most others, epitomised the dichotomous nature of the creative process. As women, they achieved creative heights at the expense of what were considered Woman's 'natural rights': love, marriage, motherhood. For these talented individuals, as art became the focus of their existence and the 'natural' world receded from their lives, this sense of alienation often turned to bitterness in their private lives. Others, often the less talented, managed to achieve some sort of a balance.

Lizzie Hudson Collier was one of these. Generous, warmhearted and sympathetic, Collier was one of Pittsburgh's leading ladies; before long, Willa Cather was visiting her backstage in both a professional and personal capacity. Yet, although the actress was clearly one of the people whom Cather idolised, she was none the less accurate in her prediction that Collier would be remembered more for her 'kindness and sympathy' than for her talent. Lizzie Collier's 'kindness' to Willa included nursing the young journalist through an attack of bronchitis; yet her real importance to Cather may be measured in other terms. It was through Collier that the 24-year-old Cather met the young woman who was to become one of the major influences of her life.

Isabelle McClung was twenty-one when she met Willa Cather some time during the theatrical season of 1898/9. She was the eldest daughter of a wealthy Pittsburgh judge, Samuel A.

McClung. Though not an artist herself, Isabelle was drawn to and was quite knowledgeable about all the arts — a Social Register girl with a Bohemian reputation. She had admired Cather's journalism for some time prior to meeting her. The two women became friends at first sight, and the relationship evolved into a loving friendship, the exact nature of which cannot be determined, for the letters they wrote to one another were destroyed shortly after Isabelle's death in 1938. There can be no doubt, however, that Isabelle McClung was the most intimate companion of Willa Cather's life; she was also a very necessary patron.

In addition to her explorations of the musical and theatrical worlds, new experiences were pouring in on Cather from all sides during the *Leader* days. In the 1899/1900 season alone she discussed nearly a hundred books, and her literary activities may be charted through the newspaper columns.

Kipling was 'a force to be reckoned with'. Yeats' *The Wind Among The Reeds* exasperated her because of its forty-three pages of accompanying notes, but *The Forest Lovers* of Maurice Hewlett proved a delight. She continued to abuse Ouida, and had a field-day with the curious *Women's Bible*, a creation of Elizabeth Cady Stanton and the Suffrage Movement. Cather was growing less scathing about women writers, however, and Kate Chopin's *The Awakening* put her at odds with herself: she did not particularly care for the story line (although she classed it as a Creole *Bovary*), but she very much admired the author — 'She writes much better than it is ever given to most people to write' — a significant tribute from one who, only four years earlier, had hardly any faith in women writers whatsoever. Zola's activities and the death of Daudet (1897) were noted, as were the works of other French writers. She discovered Housman and took him straight to heart. Eden Philpott's *Children of the Mists* pleased her a great deal; James, of course, was ever-present. There were even some opportunities to meet authors, as when she interviewed Anthony Hope Hawkins (*The Prisoner of Zenda*) in 1897.

Nevertheless, Cather felt a gnawing restlessness growing inside her. While her knowledge of the creative arts was expanding, her own creative output was minimal. Journalism had launched her, and introduced her to many famous and interesting people; she had gained a respectable reputation for her newspaper work. But the excitement had grown stale — how could one produce great things if always writing about another's success? To break the monotony, she managed a week in New York during February 1898 to see Modjeska play *Mary Stuart*, but even that was a working holiday, with part of the time spent composing reviews for the New York *Sun*.

In May she visited Washington, DC where her cousin, Howard Gore, was preparing to set off on the Wellman polar expedition. He introduced Willa to many of the capital's social circles, but it was his wife, Lillian Thekla Brandthall, who interested the young woman more than anyone else. Daughter of a Norwegian diplomat and cousin to King Oscar of Sweden, Brandthall sang Grieg melodies for Cather and read Ibsen to her. The summer of 1899 found Cather in the west, renewing family ties before returning to Pittsburgh for another year.

Then the century turned. All the frustration of unwritten hours finally reached boiling point . . . and Cather once more exploded into fiction. Fed up with the life of a newspaperwoman, she left the *Leader* in March, the same month which saw the publication of her first article in the *Library*, a short-lived literary magazine. The owner, Charles S. Clarke wanted to create a magazine similar to the London *Spectator*. Americans evidently did not care for it (the *Library* survived for just seven months) but for Cather, it was a godsend. Twenty-six items — articles, stories and poems — are known to have been published in the magazine, both under her own name and various pseudonyms. It is interesting to note that, of the twelve articles, only two bear her real name, while just one out of seven stories is pseudonymous, as is one of the seven poems. Was this a conscious decision to separate herself from journalism and make her name in literature? So it would seem, for the improved quality of her writing heralds a new era, foreshadowing the mastery which was to culminate in her novels.

Nowhere is the change more evident than in 'Eric Hermannson's Soul', first published in *Cosmopolitan* in April 1900. The story is not concerned with the new life in Pittsburgh, although some elements are present; rather, this, the first fiction of Cather's new age, derives its power from the Divide, evidently providing a release for the frustration and passion the author had kept within her for so long.

It is the story of Eric Hermannson, a handsome 'barbarian' of a Norwegian immigrant — perhaps recalling the fact that Cather had recently been entranced by her cousin's Norwegian wife. Beguiled by the minister of a fanatical religious sect, Eric initially renounces the only joy that he knows on the frontier: music, symbolised by his violin. When a visitor from the East enters his narrow existence for a few days, she plays classical music to him, such music as he has never heard before. It revitalises him and they fall in love; under her influence he breaks his vow to God and the lovers spend one glorious night dancing in each other's arms, a night which culminates in a single kiss. Next day they return to their separate hells: Eric, now damned in his own mind, to the Divide; Margaret, doomed to marriage to a grey artificial man in an environment far removed from the freedom of the Midwestern plains. Such are the bare bones of the plot but the story, of course, is much more than that.

Eric is given a splendid physical beauty, somewhat similar to that of Emil Bergson in *O Pioneers!*; there is also something of Claude Wheeler's awkwardness in him. Eric, however, is complete in his own right, perhaps the first Cather character to be seen as an individual. In him Cather has created a Siegfried of the plains who grasps a longed-for beauty only to see it twice destroyed: once, when he smashes his violin and again, when Margaret leaves him. Still, he will have his memories, even though the price is damnation. The sacrificial theme is epitomised in his words to Margaret: 'I die for you, to-night, to-morrow, for all eternity,' he tells her, knowing that not even his soul-price will allow him to have her. 'He might as well reach out his hand to take a star' — a frequent symbol of art in Cather's works. Eric 'dies' for Margaret, just as the artist must 'die' for his art.

Cather seems to have put something of herself into the character of Margaret Elliot, a restless, unsatisfied young woman who comes west for a last taste of freedom before settling into marriage. Captivated by the landscape's stark freedom, she has fantasies of living there, but her brother knows her better than she knows herself: 'You couldn't rest, even here [he tells her]. The War-cry would follow you.' It is as if the author is speaking to herself. When East and West collide, however, the result is unbridled passion. There is one scene of pure sexual power when Margaret is caught in a stampede of wild horses that threatens to throw her from her pony. Eric dives from his own saddle and forces Margaret's pony to a rock face, pinning it there by sheer strength. The herd pours past in a great, climactic wave, leaving the pony trembling, blood and foam at the bit. Afterwards, Eric declares that his love for Margaret is greater than his love for God — a declaration in direct contrast to that of Margaret's fiancé, whose supposed love letter consists of unemotional accounts of various artistic happenings; Margaret sets the letter aside with a 'slow, secret smile' just as Cather should have recognised her own true source of inspiration and set aside the second-hand world of reviews. The landscape is seen as a positive force rather than a killing power. The wide Western sky seems 'never so cold and dead and far away as in denser atmospheres' (smoggy Pittsburgh) and the scent of the cornfields is compared to that of the 'flowers of paradise'.

The myriad of emotional undercurrents contained in this story led one Dresden critic to hail it as a 'psychological masterpiece'. It was also the greatest outpouring of pure feeling that Cather had produced, as yet. The five other stories of 1900 also show a progress in creativity but none come close to the mastery of 'Eric Hermannson's Soul'.

Some time during the autumn or winter of 1900, Cather moved to Washington, DC, to try her hand at translation in a government office. She continued to freelance, sending a 'Washington Letter' to the *Journal* each week, and contributing a series entitled 'Winter Sketches in the Capital' to another magazine, *The Index of Pittsburgh Life*, which had absorbed the *Library*. That season was one of 'continuous theatre and concert going'; consequently Cather had little time left in which to write.

Willa Cather must have realised that she should give up journalism altogether. At twenty-seven, she was tired of life among the newspapers, living in boarding-houses, keeping her suitcases underneath the bed. Yet she suffered from a paralysing lack of confidence, unsure of her own ability to keep herself by her creative writing, this need for reassurance was still present even after she had become a successful novelist. At this point, however, a serendipitous Fate intervened with the offer of a vacant post at Central High School. In the spring of 1901, Cather was back in Pittsburgh, teaching Latin and living in the house of Isabelle McClung.

Evidently family quarrels erupted when Isabelle announced

her intention of having Willa as a house-guest. E.K. Brown states, cautiously, that the elder McClungs 'wondered at the propriety' of allowing Miss Cather to live in their home, although she was welcome as their daughter's friend; Byrne points to the possibility of disputes between Isabelle and her brothers and sisters. But Isabelle could be just as stubborn as her Presbyterian father. When she threatened to leave home if her friend was turned away, the family gave in. It was to have been a temporary arrangement, but in fact Cather spent the remainder of her Pittsburgh days in the fashionable Murray Hill residence — a stay amounting to more than five years.

Once again, the young woman experienced a changed set of circumstances. Gone were the communal boarding-houses with their thin walls and cooking smells. In their place was the lavishness of the McClung home, with its domestic staff, its elegant dinners and teas, which Willa might attend or not as she chose. She was also free to entertain her own friends whenever she wished. Life took on a pattern of order. The days were filled with teaching: first Latin, then (to her great relief) English. In the evenings after dinner, if there were no papers to grade, it was accepted custom for Willa and Isabelle to vanish upstairs where they could read together in peace.

Most accounts of this period agree that the two friends shared a 'room with a view' at the back of the house where they were left undisturbed. Isabelle also converted an attic sewing-room into a little study for Willa, so that she could hide away under the eaves and write with something of the old security of the Rose Bower. Safe in a family unit, relieved of financial pressures (she paid no board at the McClungs'), encouraged and nurtured by Isabelle, Willa Cather was at last able to write in peace. Many of the poems of *April Twilights* and all of the stories of *The Troll Garden* were produced at her desk in the attic.

Amid all the personal upheavals, only two poems and two stories were published that year, but the magazines in which they appeared bore the names of *Lippincott's* and *The Saturday Evening Post*. There was another trip to Nebraska that summer; Cather was always to be torn between Nebraska and the cultured East Coast. Elizabeth Shepley Sergeant tells how Cather would 'dash out to see her "family" — "my mother and father 'specially"', and then 'fly back to Pittsburgh and Isabelle McClung — for fear of dying in a cornfield'. Sergeant found this performance puzzling. 'You have not seen those miles of fields', Cather tried to explain. 'There is no place to hide in Nebraska.'

The next year witnessed a return to journalism. Although she was teaching full time at the high school — so stressful a job that she initially lost some twenty pounds in weight — it was difficult to resist the urge to freelance, and she contributed at least twelve pieces to the Pittsburgh *Gazette*, most of which were signed 'Henry Nicklemann'. Clearly, more literary writing was also receiving attention, for *Lippincott's*, *Harper's Magazine* and the *Critic* all published her poems, and *New England Magazine* printed two more stories.

The summer of 1902 found Willa and Isabelle in Europe, on that cultural Grand Tour made by so many generations of Americans. A series of travel articles helped Cather to finance the venture, as well as providing later readers with an account of the young writer's first impressions. After her journalistic interlude, Willa Cather was coming home to the Old World, a homecoming which Edith Lewis was to describe as 'more deeply moving and transfiguring than any home-coming to friends or family, to physical surroundings can ever be'.

The tour began in June on the west coast of England. From there, the friends journeyed east towards London, where they joined by Dorothy Canfield. For Cather, who had always felt an affinity towards the English, Edwardian Britain produced mixed emotions. She delighted in its history and in the countryside, revelling in the towns and villages, as well as the soft accents which made Americans sound like 'burrs on sandpaper' in comparison. Typically, little things captured most of her attention. In the article on Chester, for example, she concentrated on the ivy and climbing roses which covered the houses; the cathedral is not discussed until the very end of the piece.

Shropshire, her adored Housman's county, proved inspirational, but the want and poverty that she also saw in Britain came as a shock. It is one thing to read about toothless, stoop-shouldered street-people; quite another to see them in the flesh. She found London's flower girls and street vendors especially upsetting, and it may have been this experience that led her to invent an article. The piece in question is Cather's account of a visit to the studio of the painter Sir Edward Burne-Jones. In it, she describes in detail a conversation she had with 'James', the artist's valet — who, in fact, never existed. At the time of the visit (some four years after the artist's death) the studio had most probably been cleared out. Confronted by things in the Old World that she did not wish to see, Cather may well have fabricated the article in order to provide a little of the romance she felt *ought* to have existed. This particular fictional account was eventually incorporated into 'The Marriage of Phaedra' (1905).

The remainder of her English visit included a disastrous interview with A.E. Housman at his flat in Highgate: he mistook Willa and her companions for some expected Canadian cousins, and she was devastated to find her admired poet living in shabby bachelor quarters. Good theatre — including Beerbohm Tree's production of *The Merry Wives of Windsor* — helped to alleviate some of the disappointment she felt; but it was with relief that Willa Cather crossed the Channel to France, entering the true country of her heart.

France, to Cather, was perfect, just as it is to Claude Wheeler in *One of Ours*. She was looking for beauty everywhere; thus, it was there: in the streets of Paris (in parts, no doubt, just as dismal as parts of London); in the landscape (which bore an extraordinary resemblance to Nebraska at times); even in the cemeteries, where she walked, musing, perhaps, upon the lives of the great . . .and death, under all. Dieppe, Rouen, Marseilles, Arles; this was her own country of Passion and Romance, whose literary giants had been her lifelong companions. Provence held a special magic, and Avignon — ah, Avignon above all else was her favourite! That 'fine old city of the popes' was to provide the setting of her last, unfinished manuscript.

Only another American who has experienced it can fully appreciate what this journey must have meant to Willa Cather. To see Europe for the first time is to walk through a land dreamt of since birth, where art and history come alive each day, and greatness fills the very air. It is a discovery, the renewal of an ancient bond with the living past, a past as violent as it is beautiful. We can only guess at the full impact of this experience by examining the apparent result: within three years, Cather had published two books, the first only seven months after her return to America.

Oddly enough it was a volume of poetry. The Bostonian

Richard C. Badger, owner of the Gorham Press a vanity publisher, probably located Cather through one of the national magazines in which her work appeared. Just back from Europe with a heightened desire for solid achievement, Cather was willingly seduced by Badger's proposal that she pay part of the publication costs herself. *April Twilights*, a collection of thirty-six poems plus a 'Dedicatory', came out in the spring of 1903.

'It is a very grave question whether women have any place in poetry at all', Cather had written in 1895. Eight years later, here she was with a volume of her own. As it turned out, poetry was to be incidental to her career, but in these early days, she had earned the reputation of a capable poet, and one must agree with Slote that 'nothing in her work is unrelated to the whole'. Thus the framework for 'The Sculptor's Funeral' (1905) is laid out in the poem 'The Night Express'. 'The Namesake' prefigures the short story of that title. Some elements from 'Dedicatory' appear in both 'The Treasure of Far Island' (1902) and 'The Enchanted Bluff' (1909). In 'White Birch in Wyoming', Old World and New are synthesised through the use of Nordic and British images. The European experience is evident in many poems; Nevin shows up in at least three, and classical themes, mythology, art, death and youth form one basis of the collection.

Cather believed that women could write successful poetry only if that poetry was of a highly subjective, emotional nature; Elizabeth Barrett Browning had achieved 'merit without greatness', she said, because of her attempt to write in many styles, rather than concentrating upon and perfecting one method. She also disparaged Barrett Browning's use of classical structure and subject matter because it led to imitation. Ironically, such comments all apply to Cather herself. As with her novels and stories, her poetry was successful only when she wrote from the heart about personal subjects. Her other poems, though structually competent, are not outstanding. She, too, imitates classical poets, and the echoes of Housman are blatant, as these lines from 'In Media Vita' show:

> Herdsman abroad with his collie,
> Girls on their way to the fair,
> Hot lads a-chasing their folly,
> Parsons a-praying their prayer.

Contrast this verse with the next little poem, 'Prairie Dawn':

> A crimson fire that vanquishes the stars;
> A pungent odor from the dusty sage;
> A sudden stirring of the huddled herds;
> A breaking of the distant table-lands
> Through purple mists ascending, and the flare
> Of water ditches silver in the light;
> A swift, bright lance hurled low across the world;
> A sudden sickness for the hills of home.

Blank verse came naturally to Willa Cather; it captured the rhythm of the land she loved, as these later lines show:

> How smoothly the train runs beyond the Missouri;
> Even in my sleep I know I have crossed the river.
> The wheels turn as if they were glad to go;
> They run like running water,
> Like Youth, running away . . .

Here is the early voice of a lyric poet, preoccupied with youth and all its emotions. The mature writer was to scorn this early poetry — 'all stray copies bought up and buried' she told Elizabeth Sergeant, when that friend wanted a copy of *April Twilights*. Several critics thought the collection showed promise upon its debut, but it was a promise that was to be fulfilled in fiction.

The young Willa Cather, however, was quite pleased with her book at the time. It was, after all, an achievement (though a small one), and it belonged to 'art'. But even while she was signing copies for her admiring pupils, other events were in progress which were to shape her future course.

Back in Lincoln, Will Owen Jones was talking with H.H. McClure, who had arrived in Nebraska on a talent search for New York's McClure Syndicate. Jones asked him to examine some of Cather's early *Journal* work; H.H. did so, and then told his cousin, S.S. This latter McClure, the driving force behind *McClure's* magazine, was always on the lookout for new talent; somewhere he had come across Cather's stories and acted on a hunch. Willa Cather, however, had been previously rejected by *McClure's*, and she held no real hopes when McClure himself summoned her to his New York offices. Nevertheless, she went as soon as her teaching duties allowed (by this time she had transferred to Allegheny High School). McClure had been impressed. Upon learning that his own staff had rejected her stories, he summoned the guilty editors into his office for interrogation, and took them apart before Cather's astonished eyes. By the end of the interview, it was agreed that McClure, Phillips and Company would publish her stories in book form and it was a flabbergasted young teacher who made her way out of the office building. *The Troll Garden* was published in May 1905.

The book takes its name from one of a series of university lectures given by Charles Kingsley, entitled 'The Roman and the Teuton'. In describing the invasion of Rome by the barbarians, Kingsley compares Rome to a fairy kingdom, a 'troll garden' in which magic is constantly creating rare and beautiful objects. The forest people (Teutons) are attracted to this magic; once they have overthrown the trolls and have taken the garden, however, they discover that the magic no longer works: it has been destroyed by their own grasping desire. Cather chose another epigraph from Christina Rossetti's 'Goblin Market', a poem in which one of two sisters is seduced by goblin magic, and pines away for a further taste of forbidden fruit. Cather compared the goblin magic to that of the troll garden: both represent the effects of and struggle for the creative imagination. The seven stories of *The Troll Garden* all deal with the problems facing art and artists, contrasting culture and ignorance, East and West, true and false art, artist and 'barbarian'. Death occurs in four of the tales; 'art' eludes man's grasp in the other three — the collective effect is rather depressing, at best.

Four of the stories, while readable, are clearly inferior to the remaining three. Their subjects include a young singer, abandoned and dying in the cultural void of the West; the incompatability of marriage and art, fatal in one instance; and a would-be patroness who cannot distinguish between real and pseudo artists and art. Although the themes and settings of these tales were part of Cather's life experiences, they were not altogether her own — the ideas had engaged her mind but did not come from her heart. For this reason, they lack the feeling of stories such as 'A Wagner Matinee' (previously discussed), or of either of the two remaining stories of *The Troll Garden*.

The same experience which lay behind the poem 'The Night Express' was also partially responsible for the short story, 'The Sculptor's Funeral'. On one of her Western vacations, Willa Cather chanced to be at a railway station when a coffin containing the body of a local boy arrived; she overheard remarks to the effect that the boy had not amounted to much . . .basically because he had never been a financial success, the measure of small-town fame. Cather was all too familiar with this mentality (her own high school commencement address had received far less attention that that of a classmate's whose theme concerned private enterprise); she was to portray the attitude again and again throughout her works. In 'The Sculptor's Funeral', however, Cather has drawn what is perhaps her most biting portrait of the small-town mind gone wrong: its inability to grasp ideals, its cruel prejudices and its utter meanness.

As in the factual experience, the story opens at a railroad station: the body of a renowned sculptor has arrived 'home' to a small Kansas town, but not a single relative has come to receive it. Harvey Merrick's coffin is escorted to his childhood home by a bewildered art student, who can find no trace of his gentle mentor in the sculptor's own family. At the customary 'sitting up' with the dead, talk revolves around the money wasted on Merrick's art classes, how spoiled he had been . . . how much better to have spent the cash on lessons in business. Finally Jim Laird, a cynical lawyer who is too much of an alcoholic to escape the town he abhors, wades into this crowd of 'neighbours', and verbally dissects them. 'That is the true and eternal wonder of it anyway', Laird tells Steveans, the student, 'that it can come even from such a dung heap as this.' 'It', of course, is art.

Such prejudice, however, is not confined to small and backward towns, as Cather soon learned in Pittsburgh. In 1897 she had attended the funeral of the painter Charles Stanley Reinhart; it was poorly attended, few were present to lay him to rest. To Cather, it was sad enough that an artist should come from Pittsburgh, but the complete isolation of his death devastated her. 'I never knew the emptiness of fame until I went to that great man's funeral', she wrote. 'I never knew how entirely one must live and die alone until the day when they brought Stanley Reinhart home.' The inability of the 'barbarians' to understand and appreciate artists — or any sensitive individual — grieved

Willa Cather deeply, doubtless because she, too, felt that bitter sting within her own life. 'Single women making their way to individual destinies — who in the home circle understands them?' Elizabeth Sergeant wrote of her friend's plight. Breaking the mould was bad enough, but if the woman became a writer . . . *then* what? Out of all the stories of *The Troll Garden*, Sarah Orne Jewett picked 'The Sculptor's Funeral' as the standard to which the writer should aspire.

'Paul's Case', however, was George Seibel's choice; this story has, in the main, received more attention from critics, and Woodress states that 'Paul's Case' was the only story Cather allowed to be anthologised during her lifetime.

At first glance, the story seems to have no strong emotional roots within the author's personality; certainly the setting is divided between Pittsburgh and New York, but the plot concerns a young boy whose obsession with the theatre leads him first to robbery, then suicide. Paul, an eerie youth, has eyes of abnormal brightness; they seem to reflect an inner hysteria, with the enlarged pupils of a drug addict. He wears a fixed, unnatural smile which unnerves his teachers and only complicates their efforts to reach him. Paul's part-time job as an usher at Carnegie Hall absorbs his life totally; he lives for the theatre, and everything else seems unreal to him. When he is eventually expelled from school, his father bars him from the company of his actor friends and even makes him give up his job at the Carnegie. A 'normal', mundane job is found for him, but Paul takes matters into his own hands. He steals enough money for a nine-day spree in the dream world of New York, where he dresses in fine clothes, takes a suite at the Waldorf, attends the opera and the theatre, orders roses and champagne. When his money runs out and he faces imprisonment, Paul can find no alternative but to throw himself — immaculately dressed — under a train. For he had never wanted to be an actor: 'what he wanted was to see, to be in the atmosphere, float on the wave of it . . . away from everything'. His craving was for the world of artificial lights, shining finery, fresh flowers; in short, the world the stage presented to him.

When George Seibel read this story, he told Willa Cather that Paul seemed to be made up of two boys, a duality he says she later admitted. Byrne also points to two cousins — pupils of Cather's — as possible sources for Paul. In 1943, Cather wrote

that the main character of 'Paul's Case' had indeed been derived from two individuals, one of whom was a boy from her Latin class at Central High School. The other, however, was the author herself, especially that frustrated self who had been teaching in Pittsburg. This craving for finer things had been with her all her life. When the autobiographical Jim Burden (*My Ántonia*) attends his first real dramatic performance — *Camille*, which Cather had seen in 1893 — the effect upon him is strikingly similar to that of the stage upon Paul. The curtain opens, and Burden finds:
. . . . 'the most enchantingly gay scene I had ever looked upon. I had never seen champagne bottles opened on stage before . . . gilded chairs and tables . . . linen of dazzling whiteness, glittering glass, silver dishes, a great bowl of fruit, and the reddest of roses . . . beautiful women and dashing young men, laughing and talking together . . .'.

Willa Cather had been entranced by that atmosphere in her college days just as she was in Pittsburgh — her obsessive theatre-going has already been noted. She also recognised the potential dangers of such a passion, particularly after observing the young people she taught for five years.

Trapped in the halfway environment of Pittsburgh, with New York so near and yet so far, it is hardly surprising that the stories of *The Troll Garden* treat art as the unattainable, or as a less-than-triumphant force. Her literary career had not properly begun, but still she lacked the courage and opportunity to break free from a steady job and devote her energies exclusively to writing. Now, as a teacher, success seemed further away than ever.

And then S.S. McClure entered Cather's life for a second time, with the offer of a position on his magazine. The job meant New York and an end to teaching; it also meant leaving Isabelle and the security of the McClung household. No doubt, however, Willa Cather felt that it was high time she earned her own way again, and with McClure's dynamic charisma turned upon her, she could not resist the opportunity. Thus, the author gained New York and its atmosphere, but like Paul, she, too, paid a price: in this case, six years of her life as a writer.

5 Turning-Point

We must be ourselves, but we must be our best selves.

Letter to Willa Cather from Sarah Orne Jewett

It is all too easy to judge an artist in retrospect. Critics and biographers of Willa Cather are frequently tempted to chastise their subject for what appears to be a repetitive waste of time and talent — first, in Pittsburgh and, later, in New York at *McClure's*. Speculation springs a ready trap: what could the writer have achieved had she devoted her youthful powers more completely to her creative work? What would have resulted had she forsaken her life in Pittsburgh after only one or two years? In our admiration for the writer, we forget the woman's necessity to earn a secure living; somehow, we feel slighted for every ounce of creative blood not squeezed from her veins.

Talent, however, matures according to its own timetable. Willa Cather did not consider herself artistically mature in 1906; certainly not enough to risk going it alone. Instead she opted for the splendour of New York and the security of her position at *McClure's*. And, as she was later to tell Louise Bogan: 'I wasn't out to spy on life; I was out to live it'. At thirty-three, there was still a great deal of living to do.

Living aside, it is difficult at first glance to assess any benefits Cather may have gained at *McClure's*. Her six years as part of the magazine staff were barren, at least in one sense. Daily, her energies were channelled into the reading, editing, and rewriting of other people's work for publication — duties which effectively smothered her own creative talents. In addition, she was called upon to collaborate on projects for which she felt no enthusiasm. Elizabeth Moorhead recalled that when unwelcome assignments came her way, Willa Cather did her best to complete them with professionalism, but stipulated that her name never appear in connection with them. If a project did not interest her, or was unrepresentative of what she wanted to do, she preferred to remain anonymous. Editing was her present occupation; her true reputation lay elsewhere.

Viewed in another light, however, the sojourn at *McClure's* played a key role in the shaping of her ultimate vocation by bringing her into contact with a new friend who was to have a vital influence on her. Just as the Pittsburgh years provided Isabelle McClung, so *McClure's* led the way to Sarah Orne Jewett — certainly its most valuable contribution to Cather's career. Otherwise, the magazine had little in common with its soon-to-be managing editor.

By the time Willa Cather joined its staff, *McClure's* magazine, the brainchild of that chaotic genius, Samuel Sidney McClure, had evolved into a journalistic vehicle of hitherto undreamed of power. A pioneer of the popular magazine (selling for 15 cents as opposed to the 25 or 30 demanded by the heavier intellectual monthlies), *McClure's* led the ranks of the so-called 'muckrakers', a term coined by Theodore Roosevelt in a speech made in 1906. Although he had spoken out against corruption in politics and business, the President also resented those who profited from exposing scandal — the sort of story that *McClure's* thrived on.

Graft, fraud and injustice; the need for social and political reform . . . these were the issues which filled its pages, straight from the pens of writers such as Ida Tarbell and Lincoln Steffens. Although many articles were pure sensationalism, that sensationalism was accurate to the highest degree. Such top-rank journalism was supplemented by the 'Chief's' uncanny ability to root out the best in fiction writers on both sides of the Atlantic: Joseph Conrad, Conan Doyle, Jack London, O. Henry, even Cather's own Sarah Orne Jewett, all appeared in the magazine. This combination produced a publication of assured quality which was also succesful, whose reputation was further enhanced by the arrival of Willa Cather.

Sensationalism and social reform did not interest her in the slightest; none the less the bulk of her first two years at the magazine was spent editing and researching a lengthy manuscript about Mary Baker Eddy, the controversial founder of the Christian Science Movement (the article ran for fourteen instalments). S.S. McClure did not mind paying for accuracy as long as it increased his circulation figures; thus Willa Cather found herself dispatched to Boston on a fact-finding mission.

Even if Cather had to work upon unfavourable assignments in

the hectic world of magazine journalism, a more beneficial setting than Boston could not have been found. While New York glittered, pulsing with energy in its emergent role as the hub of the modern world, Boston remained placid and serene, wrapped in the tranquil cloak of its literary and historic past. The young woman from Nebraska must have delighted in working there, surrounded by the ghosts of her great idols. The city had been the birthplace of both Poe and Emerson. It was a regular stopping point for Charles Dickens on his American tours. Henry James had called it home for a time, and numerous writers of the famous New England School had lived in and around the Boston area. To be sure, Willa Cather was also very interested in her contemporaries, and made many new friends and acquaintances, including Ferris Greenslet of the Houghton Mifflin Company, her future publisher. As always, however, the past provided her with a sense of belonging and security, which was nowhere more evident than at 148 Charles Street, just under Beacon Hill.

It was in 1908 that Willa Cather was first taken to this address. One wintry New England day she entered a long, green-carpeted drawing room, where a tiny woman of over seventy poured tea for her. In spite of her age, the woman was enchanting, young and lively with a musical laugh. 'She did not seem old to me', Cather wrote years later. 'Frail, diminished in force, yes; but, emphatically, *not* old.' This remarkable person was Mrs Annie Fields, whose husband James had published so many of the authors Cather had loved since her childhood. During the sixty or more years that Mrs Fields lived there, the house on Charles Street became the nearest thing to a Parisian salon America had known, and the list of names of those who passed through its doors reads like a literary and artistic *Who's Who*: Dickens, Thackeray, Hawthorne, Modjeska, Sargent, Arnold, Emerson, James . . . Annie Fields had known them all, and spoke as if they had only called in an hour before. 'One came to believe that they had been very living people', Willa Cather wrote. 'At 148 Charles Street an American of the Apache period and territory could come to inherit a Colonial past.'

She had found a new haven, and visited Annie Fields as often as time allowed, both in Boston and at Mrs Fields' summer home in Manchester-by-the-Sea. As the rest of the world marched on into the twentieth century, the house on Charles Street remained firmly rooted in the Golden Age of Literature, with a woman both genteel and gentle at its centre. To Mrs Fields, Willa Cather must have appeared as some wild daughter of the plains, one who needed toning down a bit, perhaps, and educating in the arts of decorum, but one who was to be loved just the same. To Willa Cather, Mrs Fields became a beloved friend, a link to a golden era; the house itself became a sanctuary from the often bewildering modern world, a place where 'the past lay in wait for one in all the corners'.

Yet more than the past resided there. A being of the present, the cherished friend of Annie Fields, gave Willa Cather more than all the past echos and mementoes of the house put together. Sarah Orne Jewett entered Cather's life for just sixteen short months, yet her influence was profound. Cather, already an admirer of her works, felt an immediate affinity for the older, established author. It was an understandable attraction, for the two writers were startingly similar in their goals and beliefs about literature.

The 'Maine borderer', as Sarah Orne Jewett called herself, was one of the best regional fiction writers to emerge from nineteenth-century America. Yet her works were more than simply regional for, like Willa Cather's, they had been written in accordance with sound creative principles — the result of Jewett's earlier development. Like her new young friend, Jewett had steeped herself in the French and Russian novelists, and she was also well-versed in the works of Henry James. She adhered to the Arnoldian maxim of studying good writing in order to find out exactly *why* it was good; a principle that could easily have been Cather's own. Jewett also believed in writing with simplicity, and in writing from the heart — in essence, in sympathy without sentimentality, a characteristic particularly evident in her ability to evoke vivid images of her own homeland in the minds of her readers.

'She early learned to love her country for what it was. What is quite as important, she saw it as it was. She happened to have the right temperament, to see it so — and to understand by intuition the deeper meaning of what she saw.' Thus Willa Cather described her friend. The words could just as easily have been used to describe herself, although it took her years to release the love she instinctively harboured for her own 'country'. The two women shared a unique gift of sympathy in their writing, in Cather's words, the 'fine thing that alone can make [the writer's] work fine'. Such common talents, ideals, and beliefs — matured to fruition in one and yet to be developed in the other — drew the writers together. For the younger woman, Jewett assumed the role of a cherished mentor. The experienced writer recognised the stifled potential inherent in Willa Cather, and gently urged her to follow the true path of literature.

They met as often as possible, either at Mrs Fields', or at Miss Jewett's own home in South Berwick, Maine. In between times, letters flew back and forth. Willa Cather forbade publication and direct quotations from any of her letters; Miss Jewett, thankfully, did not, and the three letters to Cather which Annie Fields included in her collection (*The Letters of Sarah Orne Jewett*, edited by Annie Fields, 1911) reveal much of the relationship that existed between the writers.

The deep and tender affection Miss Jewett felt for her 'dear Willa' shows in touching admonitions: 'I wish that I could see you. . . . Send me one word on office paper to say that you are getting on well'. There is also poignant evidence of Jewett's failing health, her awareness of the passing of each moment and of time running out. Even so, she still managed to follow the progress of Cather's career.

'I wish to tell you', she wrote in the November of 1908, 'with what deep happiness and recognition I have read the 'McClure' story. . . . It made me feel very near to the writer's young and loving heart.'

From the references that follow, we may assume that the story concerned was 'On the Gull's Road', which was published in *McClure's* the following month. An extremely romantic piece, the story tells of the chance meeting of two strangers, who should have been lovers, told as a flashback. The narrator, a young man returning home to America by ship, encounters Mrs Ebbling, a Norwegian woman of failing health. She is, naturally, beautiful, and is also the wife of the ship's chief engineer, an uncaring gadabout. The two fall in love and declare themselves, yet Mrs Ebbling will not forsake her husband. Instead, she sets the young man free, presenting him with a box to open on her death: the moment when she, too, will be free. She returns to the young man his youth; he, in turn, gives her the gift of true devotion. In

Cather fashion, love is presented here as beautiful, and is allowed to blossom only because premature death will ensure that its purity remains intact.

Miss Jewett greatly admired this story and praised it highly. To her mind, it showed that Cather was truly on her way. Her one criticism, however, concerned Cather's use of a male narrator:'. . . as well done as he could be when a woman writes in the man's character'. Jewett felt that such cross-sexual styles could be nothing more than masquerades. 'You could almost have done it as yourself', she wrote. 'A woman could love her in that same protecting way — a woman could even care enough to wish to take her away from such a life.' Cather, however, continued to write through the eyes of both sexes. Always, she would be a writer first, a woman second.

At the end of this particular letter there is some timely advice from Miss Jewett: 'Do not hurry too fast in these early winter days. A quiet hour is worth more to you than anything you could do in it'. Certainly, at this point in her life, Willa Cather was constantly in need of quiet hours. Editorial duties were piling up more and more; she was forever on the move, trying to juggle a variety of responsibilities which sometimes threatened to come crashing down around her ears. Jewett knew this, and realised that such a busy and demanding life style posed a serious threat to a promising talent. Sixteen days later, she once again sat down to compose a long letter to her young friend reeling out thoughts and opinions that had obviously been troubling her for some time. It was as if she knew it was to be almost her last opportunity to do so.

First of all, she agreed that the work at *McClure's* was important, responsible and, unfortunately, incessant — the type of work which , because of its intensity, was sapping the energy of what should have been Cather's prime years of maturation. 'When one's first working power has spent itself', Jewett warned, 'nothing ever brings it back just the same.' If Cather did not take care to let her powers mature, she would never rise above the standard of stories such as 'The Sculptor's Funeral' in *The Troll Garden*.

Another point Jewett seized upon involved the question of Cather's own genre. 'I want you to be surer of your backgrounds', she explained. 'You have your Nebraska life, — a child's Virginia, and now an intimate knowledge of what we are pleased to call the 'Bohemia' of newspaper and magazine life . . .', all of which Jewett acknowledged as 'uncommon equipment'. But as she astutely pointed out, Cather was not yet objective enough to use those backgrounds to create a style and subject-matter exclusively her own.

Basically, the magazine executive was still fighting insecurity. Every artist needed reassurance, Miss Jewett told her; that was perfectly normal. But coupled with this insecurity were bouts of guilt due to the path she was then following and the neglect of what her mentor termed the 'literary conscience'. It was in order to remedy this situation that Sarah Orne Jewett gave Cather what was probably the single most important piece of advice that she ever received. Miss Jewett advocated a break with *McClure's*.

> . . . you must find your own quiet centre of life, and write from that to the world that holds offices, and all society, all Bohemia; the city, the country — in short you must write to the human heart. . . . Otherwise what might be strength in a writer is only crudeness, and what might be insight is only observation; sentiment falls to sentimentality — you can write about life, but never write life itself. . . . To work in silence and with all one's heart, that is the writer's lot; he is the only artist who must be a solitary, and yet needs the widest outlook upon the world.

'You will let me hear from you again before long?' Miss Jewett ended her missive with this innocent-sounding query, as if unaware of how this burst of philosophy would affect her protégée.

The reaction, of course, was almost immediate: an eight-page introspective reply in which Willa Cather admitted to and analysed the confusion surrounding her life. The juggling act at *McClure's* left her exhausted at the end of each day; the constant reading of inferior manuscripts had become mind-numbing, making her disgruntled and fretful. Worst of all, perhaps, McClure seemed to be trying to mould her into a journalist of the Ida Tarbell variety — and that type of writing brought her little satisfaction.

Whether unconsciously or otherwise, McClure evidently played mind-games with Cather, intimating that she would never make much of a fiction writer, but that she could be developed into a magazine executive of the first rank; an interesting assumption, considering that it was Cather's fiction which had brought her to his attention in the first place. Willa Cather must have known that her Chief only wanted to keep her for his magazine, but the added doubt eroded her already none-too-confident self-image. What if he were indeed right? Her abilities as an editor had certainly improved with experience but if she had made any *creative* progress at all during the last few years, then it had been all in her head, not on the printed page. Now, as she sat down to write, it was as if she were an infant learning from step one. Cather obviously considered leaving *McClure's*, since she admitted to Miss Jewett that if she left at that stage she would have had enough funds to allow her to live a simple existence for the next three or four years.

Why, then, did she remain at the magazine for nearly three more years? The excitement of her job and of New York (certainly she found some aspects of magazine life fascinating), her loyalty to McClure, her self-doubts, seem to be the most logical reasons. From this point onward, Cather was often troubled about her psychological state, believing that she possessed something like a split-personality. Much later in her life, she even went so far as to ask Elizabeth Sergeant whether or not she should seek psychiatric help. Duality, duality; throughout her life Willa Cather was to be tortured by divisions, doubts and differences: between man and woman, idealism and realism, present and past, art and life. For reconciliation, her only escape lay in the creative process, but each time she finished a work the problems came crowding in again. Even when she had finally become responsible for the state of her 'literary conscience' (Jewett's words), she would be plagued by doubts and be in need of a soothing voice such as Jewett's for reassurance.

Sadly, that voice was to be silenced all too soon. Sarah Orne Jewett died in June 1909 while Willa Cather was in London on another scouting mission for the magazine. Cather was devastated. Spurred on by Miss Jewett's support and criticism, she had begun several projects in the hopes of pleasing the older woman. Now, with her mentor gone, she had no authority figure to serve — it may well have been this that caused her to cling to her magazine work more than ever for security and assurance; McClure did, after all, value her work. For artistic support, there was always Isabelle McClung, with whom she had travelled to Italy in 1908. But Isabelle was not a writer, and nothing influences the apprentice so much as the voice of an established master.

Heartbreaking though it was, Miss Jewett's death did not leave Cather without companionship. During her trips abroad for *McClure's*, she had made such friends as William Archer, the London drama critic, who in turn introduced her to many members of the English literary and theatrical set, material she was later to use in her first novel, *Alexander's Bridge*.

More importantly, in September of that year she and another woman took an apartment in Washington Place. Edith Lewis was a proof-reader at *McClure's*. The two had been friends since 1903 and, although that friendship seems to have lacked the same intensity that existed between Cather and other women friends, it proved a comfortable and comforting arrangement for both parties: they shared a series of apartments for the rest of Cather's life.

There were other new faces on the horizon. The following year, Cather was interrupted at work by a rather frightened looking young woman who presented her with an article about sweated tenement workers. This was Elizabeth Shepley Sergeant, newly graduated from Bryn Mawr, very liberal, very literary, and another person Cather admitted to her close circle of friends. To Elizabeth Sergeant's youthful eyes, the managing editor of *McClure's* appeared as something of a shock. Instead of a tall, stern professional woman, here was a figure that radiated youth and buoyancy. 'Rather square', Sergeant recalls, 'her face, open, direct, honest, blooming with warmth and kindness.' There was a childishness about that face, she remembered, with its blue-grey eyes, rosy cheeks, and brown hair parted simply down the middle. Cather greeted Sergeant with an almost boyish enthusiasm, but once in her role as editor she assumed an entirely different stance. Manuscript in hand, the fresh-faced Nebraskan woman took on 'a powerful, almost masculine personality', and scanned the pages quickly and professionally. Sergeant dissolved in 'beginner's tremors', unsure what the verdict on her article would be. 'Toilers in the Tenements', however, did appear in *McClure's*; Cather did not care for the subject-matter, but it was what her Chief wanted and it was at least publishable. Thus began another friendship which was to flourish for some twenty years; after that time, the two drifted apart.

There were other friendships from different worlds: London, New York and of course, the 'folks back home', with whom Cather corresponded regularly. For the most part, though, the days merged into a blur of work — the frustrating, transient kind that left Cather dissatisfied with life in general and with herself in particular. It was an extremely difficult period, the need for some kind of decision leaving her torn between two worlds.

On the one hand lay her real need to break away, to write creatively for creation's sake; on the other hand stood McClure, a man with whom Cather maintained a working relationship based on mutual admiration and respect. Almost from the beginning, the two Midwesterners had formed an alliance of understanding. Edith Lewis remembers their relationship as being 'without a cloud'. Sergeant recalls how their very accents seemed to blend in harmony. S.S. McClure found Cather to be loyal, reliable and a good judge of quality. 'The best magazine executive I know is Miss Cather', McClure wrote to his wife in later years, when he was trying to launch a scheme for yet another publication. In turn, Willa Cather admired the charismatic, self-made, impractical man, almost to the point of hero-worship; according to Lewis, however, Cather never flattered him nor compromised her own judgement for his. Others on the magazine found their close relationship somewhat irritating. Curtis Brady, for example, who was *McClure's* business manager, wrote that Cather was considered to be a 'yes-man' by some of the office staff, as well as a generally bad influence. There can be no doubt, however, that Willa Cather's loyalty to her Chief and to the magazine helped to delay the onset of her natural career. For his part, McClure sought to keep her for himself as long as he could.

However dominating McClure sought to be, he was at least sympathetic with his managing editor. The year 1911 had opened badly for Cather, with a sudden bout of mastoiditis to add to her general unhappiness. Unable to sit still himself, McClure must have recognised the symptoms of unrest, and accordingly dispatched Cather to London once again to search for manuscripts and to have a change of scene. Had he but known, the trip was almost a herald of Cather's break with the magazine, for while in London she made more inroads into the theatrical set — experiences that would shortly be set down on paper.

74

Even so, she returned to New York still distracted and un-happy; the trip had occurred before she had fully recovered from the effects of the mastoid infection. Elizabeth Sergeant remembers Cather during this time as a 'young woman tormented by the need to become a solitary', one whose most pressing desire was 'to write life itself as Miss Jewett had done at her best'. Sergeant watched as Cather edged towards the brink, trying to muster enough courage to embrace her true calling. 'Could you do it', Sergeant recalled her friend saying, 'give yourself, dedicate yourself to your art, you who love life and find human beings so fascinating?'

While Cather wavered, debating with herself, she made a visit to Miss Jewett's home in South Berwick. There in the dear, familiar surroundings, enfolded by memories of her beloved friend, something began to reaffirm itself in Willa Cather. She felt 'goaded', she told Elizabeth Sergeant, as if her friend's spirit were reminding her that time was running out. The letter of advice had never been forgotten. Whether she began writing her first novel while still in South Berwick has not been determined, but the visit there certainly moved her to do so. By the end of the summer of 1911, *Alexander's Bridge* had been completed, and in the autumn of that year, Willa Cather took a leave of absence from the magazine. She never truly returned.

The novel which signalled Willa Cather's turning-point has been heavily criticised, not least by the author herself. Almost as soon as it appeared in 1912, Cather began to dismiss *Alexander's Bridge* as being inadequate and 'literary' — a bad word in her vocabulary. As the years progressed, her judgement of it became even more critical: she would eventually state that she had actually written two 'first novels' (*O Pioneers!* being the second). '*Alexander's Bridge* was my first novel', she wrote in the preface to the 1922 edition of the book, 'and does not deal with the kind of subject matter in which I now find myself most at home'.

By 1931, she was likening it to a 'studio picture'. The impressions in the work, she felt, were genuine but very shallow, the result of youthful enthusiasm towards new and interesting people (albeit the best handling of scenes are those in which descriptions of landscape is used). Some biographers have pointed out that, at thirty-eight, Cather was no longer youthful nor inexperienced. In one sense, this is true: she was an established magazine editor, with considerable success in short stories. As a novelist, however, she was indeed a novice, a newcomer, and as to the age at which she produced a first novel, she was in very good company: Thomas Hardy was thirty-one when his first novel was published, Joseph Conrad thirty-eight and George Eliot, forty.

Yet is was not so much her age and experience (or lack of either) that led Cather and other critics to disparage *Alexander's Bridge*. It is, in fact, a very readable and well-constructed first novel, as other biographers and critics have pointed out. What caused the most dispute was the work's actual subject matter and treatment; it did not, as Cather rightly admitted, 'belong' to her. It was contrived, in a thoroughly Jamesian fashion, and in comparison with her later novels Cather judged it to be 'superficial' and 'unnecessary'.

Stiff and formalised, yes, but certainly not 'unnecessary'. While *Alexander's Bridge* does not contain quintessential Cather, it was none the less the product of the indecision and uncertainty of her early years, when she was still trying to see her way forward. It is a novel of the head, not the heart, and as such is important for a complete understanding of its author.

The novel is concerned with Bartley Alexander, an attractive Westerner, who has made a success of his chosen profession as a builder of bridges. Together with his wife (Winifred) he has settled into a respectable Bostonian life-style — comfortable, reserved, and tragically lacking in energy. At forty-three, Alexander is in the middle of a mid-life crisis; outwardly successful, he is yet frustrated, unhappy and bewildered. Here he is talking to Professor Wilson, the observer in and narrator of the novel: 'You work like the devil and think you're getting on, and suddenly you discover that you've only been getting yourself tied up. A million details drink you dry. Your life keeps going for things you don't want, and all the while you are being built alive into a social structure you don't care a rap about'.

At the age of thirty-seven, some twenty years after her first published essay, Cather, too, felt trapped within a mould of her own making. She was a woman nearing forty who had not yet found what it was that she ultimately wanted. Her obsession with the flight of youth and energy had resurfaced — the words above were spoken by a male character, but the voice is Willa Cather's. If nothing else, *Alexander's Bridge* is a novel of frustration.

Middle age, the threat of mediocrity, the fear of an everyday existence, feelings of inadequacy . . . Alexander, like his creator, draws back in fright. 'He was not ready for it. It was like being buried alive. . . . The one thing he had really wanted all his life was to be free.' Feelings like these accompany Alexander on a business trip to London where it so chances that he meets a former lover, an Irish actress named Hilda Burgoyne. They resume their past relationship — not so much because of the passion between them, but because through Hilda Alexander can briefly recapture his lost youth, which haunts him throughout the story like a *Doppelgänger*. Ah, youth, youth! This is what Alexander lacks, and here Cather uses for the first time a theme which runs through the work of her maturity like a refrain: youth as the essence of life, together with a nostalgia for the lost, golden days of the past: '. . . how glorious it [youth] had been, and how quickly it had passed; and when it passed, how little worthwhile anything was'.

Alexander begins to lead a double life which, predictably, leads to his downfall. Unable to resolve the split within himself, he procrastinates about taking a decision, in the process neglecting his professional responsibilities — the most important being a monumental bridge under construction in Canada. Just when he has finally decided to leave Winifred for Hilda, even though he still loves his wife in his own way, a structural fault develops in the bridge. Alexander, with the letter setting out his intentions in his pocket, rushes to the bridge, only to die when it collapses beneath him. The letter never reaches Winifred; his reputation is saved by death. Like his bridge, Bartley Alexander has collapsed under the weight of a double existence, due to his own 'structural fault'.

Cather's frustration at not having enough from life; her preoccupation with her psychological state, principally split-personality; the present environments of Boston and London; her last homage to Henry James . . . all these elements and more (including an actual bridge disaster in Canada) went into the making of *Alexander's Bridge*. *McClure's* published it in instalments as 'Alexander's Masquerade' beginning in February 1912. Houghton Mifflin brought it out in book form under the original title in April of that year, and a British edition was published by Heinemann. The completion of the book acted like a catharsis on

Willa Cather; it set her free to leave both it and *McClure's* behind and to move on towards her destiny as a writer of novels. One can view the work as a prelude to the true melody of her real voice.

Her decision could not have been better timed. *McClure's* was in the throes of yet another financial shake-up in which the spendthrift S.S. finally lost control of his empire. Cather resigned as managing editor, not without some feelings of guilt at leaving her adored Chief alone to face his enemies. Although she fully intended to stay on as a staff writer, she took a much-needed leave of absence from the office. Beginning in the autumn, she and the beloved Isabelle rented a house in the peaceful surroundings of Cherry Valley, New York.

It was not an immediate vacation. First, she dutifully set about making some necessary cuts and revisions of *Alexander's Bridge* for *McClure's*' Cameron Mackenzie who, together with Fred Collins, was now in charge of the magazine's editorial side. It was a job Cather performed without any enthusiasm, for by this time two new stories were taking shape. As with most writers, once she had completed a project she immediately lost interest in it; it became static, a dead thing. The next story was always the one that mattered.

And these new projects mattered a great deal. The first fragment, 'Alexandra', was never published; instead, it eventually became part of *O Pioneers!*, Cather's second 'first novel'. As soon as she had finished 'Alexandra', Cather started into another story, 'The Bohemian Girl', with which she was quite pleased, but felt sure no magazine would touch. She told Elizabeth Sergeant that the story was unlike anything she had written before, but she liked it all the same. Would Sergeant mind looking at it for her?

Elizabeth Sergeant read the manuscript and was at once convinced that 'this was it': finally, Willa Cather had produced a story true to herself and to her potential. Sergeant was so excited by this revelation that she rushed to New York to congratulate her friend, much to Cather's astonishment. They spent the best part of the next two days arguing about the value of the story, Elizabeth Sergeant convinced of its worth, Willa Cather remaining dubious. Soon after her return to Massachusetts Sergeant received a letter from Cather. She had lunched with Cameron Mackenzie, she wrote, who took possession of the story in spite of Cather's protests of unsuitability. Next day, over tea at the

Brevoort, Mackenzie offered her $750 for it. Willa Cather, startled, said that no one knew better than she that *McClure's* never paid more than $500 for a story. Mackenzie told her to stop being a goose; even made her promise to take more for the next one. Thus 'The Bohemian Girl' was published in the August issue of *McClure's*.

The story, as James Woodress so rightly claims, is 'vintage Cather'. Nils Ericson, the sole wanderer in a large Midwestern immigrant family, has returned to his boyhood home on the Divide after a long absence. The love he feels for the land itself is instantly rekindled. His mother and brothers, however, have all become part of the new wave of self-satisfied land-owners, whose values revolve around material possessions. They denigrate the 'old ways' and the traditions of their fathers; indeed, they appear as a rather dull lot, with fixed views and closed minds. The only livelier members of the community are some of the older generation of immigrant women, and Clara Vavrika and her father. Clara, Nils' former love, has married Olaf, the most unimaginative of his brothers, but somehow has managed to retain her naturally wild, free spirit. She is completely unsuited for life on a Nebraskan farm: craving music, passion and romance, she answers Nils' renewed summons by running away with him.

With its portrayal of immigrant types and contrasting values, 'The Bohemian Girl' foreshadows many elements of *O Pioneers!* Perhaps more striking than the portrayal of the characters themselves, however, is the treatment of and emphasis upon the land itself. Cather, at thirty-eight, was finally able to come to terms with her landscape. Just as Nils renews his love for it by a return, so, too, would his creator: her fee for 'The Bohemian Girl' helped to pay for a visit to the Southwest and Cather was off to visit her brother Douglass in Arizona. Afterwards, she was never to be the same. She had written of a wanderer's return to his country; in doing so she unwittingly paved the way for her own return to the past, and thus laid the foundations for her future.

'A reporter can write equally well about everything that is presented to his view', Cather wrote, 'but a creative writer can do his best only with what lies within the range and character of his deepest sympathies.' Free at last from both reportage and imitation, Willa Cather was about to discover exactly where her own deepest sympathies lay.

6 Arrival

> There is a time in a writer's development when
> his 'life line' and the line of his personal endeavor
> meet. This may come early or late, but after it
> occurs his work is never quite the same.
>
> from Preface to *Alexander's Bridge*, September 1922

In an interview that she gave in 1921, Willa Cather maintained
that she never travelled to the West merely to gather material for
her stories. 'I don't even come west for local color,' she declared
and, on a conscious level at least, that assertion may well have
been true. But as she herself admitted during the same interview,
such trips did in fact furnish her with what she called 'inspiration'. And although the comments at the time were centred upon
her childhood home in Nebraska, they would come to embrace
the whole of the American West.

Oddly enough, this country of inspiration was never a world in
which she could physically remain. Certainly she could not write
there for any length of time; she was much too close to the source.
Even so, throughout her life Willa Cather remained torn between
her two worlds, and the West — particularly the Southwest —
always had the power to draw her. The land served her as a
muse, providing the vital spark needed to unleash all the
suppressed natural passion she had harboured for a wild land
and its people since her days as a girl in Webster County.

Now that frustration and imitation had both been written away
with the death of Bartley Alexander, Cather could board her
train for Arizona with a purged mind. The joyful sensation of
working with material more natural to her still lingered from
'The Bohemian Girl', and she was ready for new impressions. In
the spring of 1912, then, she set off to visit her brother Douglass.
Over the course of the next fifteen years, Willa Cather was to
make five such journeys to the Southwest, each one providing
'inspiration', as well as contributing actual incidents to her
works. This particular return/encounter, however, proved both
reviving and invigorating; so much so that it may stand as the

classic example of the Catherian translation process. Consciously she may not have been idea-gathering, but unconsciously the entire journey found its way into her writing.

The shock of an unknown land, stark, bleak in its contrast, had forced open the awareness of the child Willa. For the mature woman, returning after years of absence, the effect was much the same. Back in the East and insulated in its civilized layers, she had remembered only the pungent flavour of the land. But here, meeting it head on, she was once more overawed by the vast distances, the consuming greatness of it all. At close quarters that awe turned to anxiety; she was plagued once again by irrational fears of being swallowed up in miles of cornfields. Remove her from the vastness, however, and that reaction mellowed considerably.

In *O Pioneers!*, the first novel Cather completed after these travels, it is the land that is the hero. At the end of the story its human counterpart, Alexandra Bergson, speaks to her friend and husband-to-be, Carl Linstrum. She would like to see other places but never to stay away from the Divide forever; for her, freedom lies in its soil, and no one realizes this more than Carl. 'You belong to the land', he tells her, 'now more than ever.' Alexandra agrees — she has always been its extension — but something greater radiates from this grass country; something eternal and enduring. 'The land belongs to the future', she says at last. 'We come and go, but the land is always here. And the people who love it and understand it are the people who own it — for a little while.'

In *The Song of the Lark*, the novel written after *O Pioneers!*, Cather extends this eternal quality by linking the country to the past. As Ray Kennedy's party (Thea Kronborg included) travels out beyond Moonstone towards the sand hills they experience sensations of retreating from the present, of moving backwards in time, particularly when they encounter a mirage.

> Every rabbit that shot across the path, every sage hen that flew up on the trail, was like a runaway thought, a message that one sent into the desert. As they went farther, the illusion of the mirage became more instead of less convincing; a shallow silver lake that spread for many miles, a little misty in the sunlight. Here and there one saw reflected the image of a heifer, turned

loose to live upon the sparse sand grass. They were magnified to a preposterous height and looked like mammoths, prehistoric beasts standing solitary in the waters that for many thousands of years actually washed over that desert: the mirage itself may be the ghost of that long-vanished sea.

By the time *My Ántonia* appeared a few years later, the sentiment of vastness and timelessness had assumed an even more spiritual aspect. After young Jim Burden recovers from the initial shock of his encounter with the land (Chapter 2, above), he becomes reconciled to it, almost revelling in it as he lies in a field: 'At any rate, that is happiness; to be dissolved into something complete and great. When it comes to one it comes as naturally as sleep'. Six years of time and distance were required before fear could turn to happiness.

In 1912, however, Willa Cather did not in the least enjoy being 'dissolved' into the landscape and when she at last arrived in Winslow, Arizona, during April, the prospects for happiness seemed even less promising. The town Douglass Cather called home was nothing more than a desert shanty town, strewn with tin cans and other rubbish. To make matters worse, her brother shared his tumbledown house with an inarticulate brakeman named Tooker, whose English seemed to have been learned almost entirely from magazines. Ever prone to snap judgements, Cather at first thought Tooker unbearable. Added to this scenario was an alcoholic Englishman who cooked and kept house for the railroadmen. How her brother could ever have imagined she could work in such surroundings was a mystery to Willa Cather, and she apparently made up her mind to cut her stay short and leave after only a couple of weeks. When she encountered the desert itself, however, the world took on an entirely different aspect.

Out beyond dirty little Winslow lay unexplored vistas: Indian missions, Walnut Canyon, aboriginal cliff dwellings and, finally, the Grand Canyon itself. The first days of boredom gave way to others filled with horseback rides, hiking and climbing. Willa Cather began to live out a childhood dream with Douglass as they rambled through the countryside, fulfilling the plans they made as children with Roscoe to explore the Southwest together someday. Away from town, even the awkward Tooker proved more agreeable, for he shed his artificial litany and began to talk naturally, telling marvellous stories. Soon Douglass was declaring that his sister was wearing them all out with her insatiable demands for exploration; they spent weeks making dawn to dusk excursions, returning to the civilization of hotel beds only when evening drove them back. After the toil and drudgery at *McClure's*, Cather was having the time of her life. Predictably, such new and exciting experiences were destined to appear in print.

Elements of Tooker's personality are to be found in Ray Kennedy of *The Song of the Lark* ('Occasionally he used newspaper phrases, . . . but when he talked naturally he was always worth listening to'), while the down-at-heel English cook is translated into Henry Atkins of 'Tom Outland's Story' in *The Professor's House*. The canyon hikes and cliff dwellings were also to figure heavily in both these tales (Walnut Canyon becomes Thea's 'Panther Canyon' in *The Song of the Lark*), and their images would be reinforced and supplemented by a second visit in 1915. On this first trip Cather wrote to Elizabeth Sergeant that she had also become conscious of a certain spirituality in the West; it was in Winslow that she first encountered Catholic priests and admired the tact and feeling with which they handled their Mexican and Indian parishioners — prophetic statements that Elizabeth Sergeant was to recall years later when *Death Comes for the Archbishop* came into her hands.

The Mexican community was an experience in itself. Douglass Cather, like Emil Bergson of *O Pioneers!*, had grown to love these people as he travelled through parts of Mexico, spending enough time there to gain a fair command of Spanish. Soon, through his introduction, he found his sister completely infatuated with Julio, a Mexican from Vera Cruz, a young, bronzed singing Antinous, who took her to a Mexican dance where she was the only Anglo present. Part of Julio's personality remains in the *Lark's* 'Spanish' Johnny Tellamantez, and certainly Thea's dance with the Mexicans in the same novel is derived from this experience.

Even small incidents rarely failed to leave an impression. From Julio, Cather learned the Aztec legend of 'The Forty Lovers of the Queen'; several years later, the same legend would find an unlikely place in 'Coming, Aphrodite!', a short story published in *Youth and the Bright Medusa* (1920).

In an interview she gave in 1913, Cather defined imagination, that quality of a writer's life-blood, as 'a response to what is going on — a sensitiveness to which outside things appeal . . . a composition of sympathy and observation'. All her life, Willa Cather had subconsciously observed and responded to the world about her by sifting and committing experiences to memory — all those experiences which particularly attracted her sympathy. These would come back to her in another form, flowing from her pen so quickly and so easily that often she did not recognise them as actual past events; she believed them to be products of invention, until someone else proved otherwise. For example, after the publication of *My Ántonia* in 1918, Charles Cather pointed out several incidents within the story that were derived from events that occurred during the author's Red Cloud days. 'Daughter' was taken aback: she had been convinced that they were all of her own creation. In later years she would admit to her source material more and more (at least if it pertained to setting or history), even telling an interviewer in 1921 that: 'A book is made with one's own flesh and blood of years'. Sympathy, observation and experience; for Willa Cather, that was imagination indeed.

One could observe for only so long, however, could amass only so much experience. After two months spent exploring the countryside, Cather had had her fill of the Southwest for the time being. One hot desert day, feeling strangely melancholy, she sat outside a New Mexico village, puzzling over her mood by the muddy Rio Grande. Looking down at the sandy earth, a long-forgotten sentence from Balzac flashed before her eyes:

Dans le desert, voyez-vous, il y a tout et il n'y a rien — Dieu, sans les hommes.

(In the desert, you see, there is everything and there is nothing — God, without men.)

Even inspiration, devoid of creative output, proved sterile, a static thing. It was time to go back home to the East, where objective distance would allow creativity to empty itself once again.

First, however, Cather made a stop *en route* in Red Cloud where, for the first time in years, she was able to witness the wheat harvest. If the Southwest possessed one type of grandeur, the native plains of the Divide produced their own special stimulus. It was on the edge of a wheat field, Cather told Elizabeth

Sergeant, that a new story, 'The White Mulberry Tree', had suddenly come to her. She planned to start work on it immediately she returned to Pittsburgh. Meanwhile, she had written a poem in an attempt to capture one impression that the landscape had made on her:

> Evening and the flat land,
> Rich and sombre and always silent;
> The miles of fresh-plowed soil,
> Heavy and black, full of strength and harshness;
> The growing wheat, the growing weeds,
> The toiling horses, the tired men;
> The long empty roads,
> Sullen fires of sunset, fading,
> The eternal unresponsive sky.
> Against all this, Youth,
> Flaming like the wild roses,
> Singing like the larks over the plowed fields,
> Flashing like a star out of the twilight;
> Youth with its insupportable sweetness,
> Its fierce necessity,
> Its sharp desire,
> Singing and singing,
> Out of the lips of silence,
> Out of the earthy dusk.

Entitled 'Prairie Spring', the poem was to serve as an epigraph for *O Pioneers!* Yet, written as it was before the conception of that novel had formed completely in the author's mind, 'Prairie Spring' carried an aura of prophecy. Its images suggest an eternal, dichotomous landscape — newly civilized and yet ancient; harsh, indifferent, and yet beautiful. Next follows the vision of youth and its passions; the larks, the flashes of starlight and the singing, are almost too coincidental, when one considers the appearance of the story of Thea Kronborg, three years later. Finally, by invoking' both images — brooding landscape and passionate youth — the poem presents a synthesis, an embodiment, the creation of a fused whole. In this first response to her return to the Southwest, Willa Cather foreshadowed the themes which were soon to ripen into what are generally acknowledged to be her most triumphant works: *O Pioneers!* (1913), *The Song of the Lark* (1915), and *My Ántonia* (1918).

The spark for each was to be ignited by Cather's response to events taking place in her own life: a return to the land of her youth; her acquaintance with a prima donna; the rediscovery of an old friend. Yet all three are rooted both in Cather's past and in her new-found, newly-released passion for the landscape. As each idea presented itself, she realized that here was material of *her* making, *her* inspiration. Like her character, Alexandra, Willa Cather was to be the first woman writer to turn a face towards the American plains with true feeling, the first to write about it with pure passion. It was precisely that passion, following no guidelines but those of her own creative instinct, which was to set both the author and the state of Nebraska on the map of American literature.

Cycle of Triumph: the Immigrant/Found Tales

The three books mentioned above were the result of Cather's first encounter with the material she was to make her own; as such, they form the first cycle within the whole framework of her novels. Considered as a triptych, this phase of Cather's writing is characterised by the growth of a new land, the energy and passion of its foreign settler-immigrants, and nostalgia for the recent past. It began with *O Pioneers!*

When Willa Cather left the West after her first glorious sojourn, she immediately returned to the McClung residence in Pittsburgh to give form to all the new ideas jostling her mind. She began with the story that had come to her during the wheat harvest, a romantic tale of two ill-fated young lovers; she called it 'The White Mulberry Tree'. She then returned to 'Alexandra', the other, rather cool piece composed the previous autumn. What happened next has been described as an 'inner explosion and enlightenment': the two stories were woven together, and by the December of 1912 *O Pioneers!* had been created. As Cather explained in later years, she had written the book to please herself and was genuinely surprised when others found it interesting.

For one thing, the story is set in Nebraska, a location she mockingly described as 'distinctly déclassé' as a literary background. Moreover, the story line had no definite skeleton or structure — the one flaw Elizabeth Sergeant pointed out and which Cather admitted. All the same, as she told Sergeant, in the landscape that insisted upon being the novel's hero, there were no sharp edges; the black earth was soft, and life fell into place without a particular pattern. The land itself had no definite skeleton, thus neither did the plot. If it was, perhaps, her most foolish endeavour yet, at least it was her most honest one. For that reason the book was dedicated to Sarah Orne Jewett.

O Pioneers! (the title is taken from Whitman's poem) portrays the growth of a new country and its people. The reader watches as the pioneer state of Nebraska moves through its early hardships of drought and crop failures towards the expansion of material success on the edge of the twentieth century. The saga (for saga it is — the novel has truly heroic overtones) unfolds around the figure of Alexandra Bergson, oldest child of a family of Swedish immigrants who have come to make a life in the New World and have settled on the Divide. When her father dies in the 1880s Alexandra takes charge of the farm's affairs. Over the years, through her love for the country, her imagination and a great deal of foresight, she manages to turn it from a debt-encased smallholding into a successful farming empire. Often Alexandra's talents bring her into conflict with two of her brothers, Otto and Lou, who — though loyal and hard-working — have no great intelligence or insight; they eventually emerge to join the growing numbers of the new American materialist generation by the novel's end.

Throughout the story Alexandra is a solitary figure; her labours of love for the country and her adherence to and respect for older, more moral values cost her her youth. Her only hope for the future lies in her youngest, son-like brother Emil, the most Swedish in temperament, whom she sees as her heir. Yet these hopes are dashed when Emil finally yields to his passionate love for Marie Tovesky, a childhood sweetheart; found embracing under a tree, the two are killed by Marie's jealous husband. At the end of the novel an old friend of Alexandra, Carl Linstrum, finally returns to marry her, but the marriage is one of comfort rather than passion. The land, as Cather had foreseen, emerges as the true victor, an eternal entity of which Alexandra seems to be an extension; a temporary embodiment, she will eventually be absorbed back into the soil, as the final lines testify: 'Fortunate country, that is one day to receive hearts like Alexandra's into its bosom, to give them out again in the yellow wheat, in the rustling corn, in the shining eyes of youth!'

On another level, however, though not as yet clearly defined, the figure of Alexandra shows Cather's first portrayal of the pioneer as artist. She is a woman who has helped create a country from an ideal. It is because Alexandra works with ideas that she is successful, as Cather states at the beginning of the novel: 'A pioneer should have imagination, should be able to enjoy the idea of things more than the things themselves.' It is this quality which sets Alexandra apart from her ant-like brothers, who are able only to toil, and never see what lies behind the work itself.

All of Cather's protagonists exhibit this characteristic of *striving*; all share in the search for an ideal. Some, like Bartley Alexander, either search in the wrong direction (as he for his lost youth), or are too preoccupied with the search itself and miss the ideal altogether, as Claude Wheeler in *One of Ours*; thus they perish. Others, like Alexandra, have identified their aims and are strong enough to reach them. But triumph is always bought at a price: Alexandra's success is surely bittersweet.

The first of Willa Cather's triumphant sagas, *O Pioneers!* served to establish its creator. It appeared in the United States in 1913, and William Heinemann, who had published her previous work, brought out a British edition. Despite the author's fears, the book was a decided success: her friends liked it, as Sergeant had predicted; the critics were kind. Most importantly of all, however, the people of Red Cloud and the Divide found it true to heart. This was a real satisfaction for Willa Cather for, despite her self-imposed exile from the territory, one liked to please the home folks now and then. The overall response was a definite boost to her confidence; her method had been individual and honest and it had worked!

Meanwhile, her personal life was also taking a turn for the better. Earlier that autumn, Edith Lewis had discovered a spacious apartment at Number 5 Bank Street, New York, and now that the book was out of the way, Willa herself was ready to move into it. It was to be her base for fifteen years, the most permanent home she had known since Red Cloud. Seven large rooms with high ceilings and big windows provided enough space for both privacy and entertaining; with the addition of some simple furniture and Josephine Bourda, a French cook who refused to speak English, the atmosphere was perfect. Now, at last, Willa Cather could settle down and deal properly with her writing.

First, however, she performed a labour of love for S.S. McClure, by ghosting his *Autobiography*. The volume was written to help the reckless dynamo out of debt with the magazine's new owners. Cather enjoyed the exercise and performed it for nothing, doubtless easing her conscience somewhat for having left the Chief behind. In addition to this duty, she also agreed to produce a series of articles for the new *McClure's*, including one set devoted to opera singers. Two were American: Louise Homer of Pittsburgh and Geraldine Ferrar of Massachusetts. The third was more intriguing: a Swedish-born immigrant who was then the leading Wagnerian soprano at New York's Metropolitan Opera House. Soon Elizabeth Sergeant received letters brimming over with Fremstad, wonderful Fremstad — clearly the woman behind the name had touched a vital nerve in Cather, and one could almost see a new story beginning to form.

Willa Cather first encountered Olive Fremstad in early 1913, when she made an appointment to interview the soprano for the magazine article. The prima donna arrived pale and exhausted after a slight automobile accident, her magnificent voice reduced to a painful whisper. Cather excused herself and arranged to return another time. That same evening she, Edith Lewis and Isabelle McClung attended a performance of *Tales of Hoffmann* at the Met — just one of their many opera evenings. When an announcement revealed that the principal soprano had been taken ill, and that Fremstad had agreed to step in at the last moment, Willa Cather steeled herself for what was sure to be a fiasco. Fremstad, however, rose to the occasion triumphantly, completing the opera with a voice of miraculous quality. Remembering their earlier encounter, Cather was dumbfounded. 'But it's impossible', she repeated to Edith Lewis, 'it's impossible'. Through the subsequent interviews that finally materialized, Olive Fremstad became not only a friend; she also formed the core of a new novel that had begun to take shape in Cather's mind.

It would be some time before the concept came to fruition. She spent that summer on her last commercial work for *McClure's*, and afterwards she and Isabelle journeyed through the Shenandoah Valley. It was October before Cather was once more ensconced at the McClungs' and working fervently upon her new novel. Some two years and 200,000 words later, Houghton Mifflin published *The Song of the Lark*.

Edith Lewis would afterwards write that none of Cather's characters was more fictitious than Thea Kronborg, the *Lark's* heroine. At a first glance this may appear to be so. The story chronicles the life of Thea, daughter of a Swedish family, from her beginnings in a small Colorado town, to her struggles through music studies in Chicago and the awakening of her true vocal talents and, finally, shows her success as a diva in New York.

Yet one must follow Lewis's statement to completion. On the 'inner level', she said, 'the person who most resembled Thea Kronborg in thought, in feeling, in spiritual development, is Willa Cather herself'. As Olive Fremstad exclaimed, joyously, when she read the book, she didn't know where Cather ended and she herself began. For Thea, though fictitious, is a composite character, created from the stuff of Cather's memories and her own passionate struggles, overlaid with Fremstad's personality and music. In some places the overlay is quite translucent, and it is difficult to separate the character's experiences from those of the author.

For example, the crowded household in which Thea grows up is set in 'Moonstone, Colorado', but the description is that of Willa's own house in Red Cloud. A strong mother, full of insight; a vague but loving father who is unaware of his daughter's talents; the worn out German piano teacher; the miscellaneous citizens of Moonstone; a sympathetic, romantic doctor . . . these are the figures which peopled Cather's childhood. Even her old room, the sacred Rose Bower, is recreated for Thea as a budding artist's sanctuary.

Thea, too, feels the same struggles as Willa Cather had felt in adolescence; she knows that same strange yearning for distant splendour, and later feels the tortuous dichotomy it brings. Like Cather, she is torn between her love for the backward little town and its people and her love for the pursuit of her art. 'She felt as if she were being pulled in two, between the desire to go away forever and the desire to stay forever.' Her turning-point is Cather's own. After wearing herself to a shadow in Chicago with her music lessons, teaching and singing she is swept away just in time to Arizona, where she can rest, recuperate and come to

90

terms with herself. Here are the familiar cliff dwellings, which give an added dimension to her own past; here is the landscape, with its eternal quality; it is here that she decides to follow her true vocation to its end. Afterwards nothing — not even her mother's illness — stops Thea in the pursuit of her art. When at last she reaches the twin pinnacles of fame and achievement, when she has become 'Kronborg', Thea, not unexpectedly, finds the taste of success to be bittersweet. The god of the art demands human sacrifices, and Thea tells her life-long friend Dr Archie that it is 'like being woven into a big web. You can't pull away, because all your little tendrils are woven into the picture. It takes you up, and uses you, and spins you out; and that is your life. Not much else can happen to you.'

None the less, achievement does somehow synthesize matters for the artist. It is *because* of her simple background and love of home truths that Thea has become the great 'Kronborg': 'They save me: the old things,' she says, 'things like the Kohlers' garden. They are in everything I do.' A related note of nostalgia is struck at the end of the novel, when Cather makes Thea agree with the Wagnerian maxim that art is a way of remembering youth; the older one becomes, the more precious it seems. Cather knows that a return to the past is not possible, yet she makes Thea cling to it all the same — just as she herself was to do. In 1914, the outbreak of the First World War had awakened Willa Cather's sense of panic about the future, causing her to look back over the previous years with even greater love than before. Elizabeth Sergeant recalled that, from the onset of the war, her friend kept repeating a mournful little maxim: 'Our present is ruined — but we had a beautiful past.' Alexandra had said that the land belonged to the future; Thea, however, so much closer to Cather's own personality, looks back to the past for solace.

Willa Cather chose to inscribe her new novel to Isabelle McClung, with the following short poem as its epigraph:

On uplands,
At morning,
The world was young, the winds were free;
A garden fair,
In that blue desert air,
Its guest invited me to be.

How fitting that a story of an artist's struggle towards perfection should be dedicated to one who had so often urged that perfection onwards. In addition to numerous short stories, most of *O Pioneers!* and *The Song of the Lark* had been written in the attic sanctuary of the McClung household.

The title of this latter work comes from a French painting Willa Cather had seen hanging in the Chicago Art Institute: a young peasant girl stops to hear a lark singing as she is crossing some fields. The title of the book was meant, Cather said, 'to suggest a young girl's awakening to something beautiful'.

Though full of passion and more structured than the story of Alexandra Bergson, the *Lark*, as Cather later realized, suffers not only from too much detail but also from being too long. In her preface to the 1932 edition, the author admitted that the book's main fault was its descending curve, and that the height of Thea's achievement was not nearly so interesting as her struggle. William Heinemann refused to publish the book for similar reasons: ' . . . he thought in that book I had taken the wrong road, and that the full-blooded method, which told everything about everybody, was not natural to me', Cather recalled in 1931, and by that time she agreed with him. When the novel was reissued the following year, she cut nearly 7,000 words.

Despite its anticlimactic ending and faults of length, *The Song Of The Lark* is a very effective, emotional novel, full of insight into the lives of all artists, with their common passions. It is also a splendid rendering of youthful longing and struggle.

The completion of any novel always left Willa Cather sunk in post-creative depression. She had been living with Thea Kronborg for the better part of two years, and by the time the novel appeared in 1915 she was in need of a change to rid her system of the Swedish singer. Again S.S. McClure appeared, and tried to recapture her with a proposal to do some kind of journalism in Germany (he was at that time editor of the *New York Evening Mail*). Isabelle McClung was to have accompanied Willa to Europe, but Judge McClung held the purse strings and refused his daughter permission. There seems to have been some sort of altercation here, which may well have been a prelude to Isabelle's impending announcement of her engagement — a fact that devastated Cather when she was told of it during the winter of 1915/16. Whatever the cause, Willa Cather refused McClure's summons and headed west once again, this time with Edith Lewis as her companion.

Their first destination was in southwestern Colorado's Mesa Verde, another location out of Cather's childhood dreams. At that time, Mesa Verde was still in the process of excavation, and its numerous prehistoric cliff dwellings had been open to the public for less than a decade. During this trip Cather called on one of the Wetherills, brother to the Dick Wetherill who had swum the Mancos river and stumbled upon the cliff dwellings — his is Tom Outland's tale in *The Professor's House*. Cather and Lewis were taken into the dwellings by an inexperienced guide; they were lost for a short period as a result, but the adventure was pure pleasure for both women, especially for Willa, who was falling in love with the country. Edith Lewis had ample opportunity to observe her friend's relationship to the land, both in Colorado and during the latter part of their journey in Taos, New Mexico.

'She was intensely alive to the country', Lewis remembered. 'She did not talk about it much but one felt that she was deeply engaged with it always, was continually receiving strong impressions from the things she saw and experienced.' It was not a purposeful storing up, however, for Cather loved the country for its own sake. But as always, the objects of Cather's love were destined for her writing; as she told Elizabeth Sergeant, one was captive to the regions and persons one loved — neither could ever be left behind. 'We are what we love', she said pleadingly, 'that is all we are.'

It is perhaps this trait — a great capacity for deep feeling — that makes Willa Cather's novels so evocative and so alive. But that same love, when worked upon by her old enemy, change, could also cause her great despair. For Cather there had been too many changes of late.

To begin with, the War, to which she seemed oblivious on the surface, was affecting her quite deeply. On subsequent visits to Red Cloud and the surrounding country, Cather witnessed at close range the conflicting loyalties of the Divide folk; she grieved, too, for so many bright young lives that were destined to be wasted. All these emotions were to re-surface in *One of Ours*. On a more personal front, changes were also coming thick and fast: Annie Fields had died during the early part of 1915. In November of that same year, Isabelle's father, Judge McClung, passed away, and his death meant the end of the Murray Hill house, which would surely be sold. Willa and Isabelle spent a last, dismal Christmas there together, but the upset caused by the loss of Judge McClung was only a prelude to an even greater shock: shortly after the holiday Isabelle revealed her plans to marry Jan Hambourg, a concert violinist. To Willa Cather, this news meant the end of the most intimate friendship of her life, and the effect of this blow lasted for months. Stunned, shattered, she broke the news desperately to Elizabeth Sergeant: 'Her face — I saw how bleak it was', Sergeant recalled. 'All her natural exuberance had drained away.' For solace, Willa fled westward once again, to the landscape of her heart and to the comfort of her brother Roscoe and his family. From there she was summoned to Red Cloud to help nurse her mother out of a serious illness.

Taking over all the household chores (including cooking for eight) was salutary after the Isabelle crisis. Cather took great pleasure and comfort in getting back into the swing of everyday life, where people still thought of her as 'Willie'. Her competence and enthusiasm over what some would call mundane matters usually astonished both friends and admirers, but it was as indigenous to her own character as it was to those of her pioneer heroines, who could pull a plough, bake bread and dance with equal aplomb. On his first encounter with Willa Cather in 1924, Burton Rascoe recognized this ability immediately. 'Miss Cather looked', he wrote, 'as though she might conduct a great law practice or a successful dairy farm, superintend a telephone exchange or run a magazine with equal efficiency, ideas and energy.' She was always to retain some part of that pioneer efficiency, and it will come as no surprise to the reader to learn that when she returned from her domestic interim, she brought with her the first chapters of a novel about the third and greatest of her heroines.

Once, while still recovering from Isabelle's defection, Willa called on Elizabeth Sergeant, who had recently moved to New York. Suddenly during the course of the conversation (on Henry James, as usual) Cather paused and placed an apothecary jar full of orange and brown flowers in the centre of a bare table.

'I want my new heroine to be like this', she said, 'like a rare object in the middle of a table, which one may examine from all sides. I want her to stand out like this — like this' — she pulled over a lamp as a spotlight — 'because she *is* the story.' So saying, her eyes filled with tears. Sergeant asked if she were thinking of someone from the past; Cather nodded but would say no more. Whether the 'someone' was Lyra Garber or Annie Sadilek we do not know; it is a fact, however, that the latter came back with her to New York, in the guise of Ántonia Shimerda.

No single work (with the possible exception of 'Old Mrs Harris') contains so many clearly traceable elements of Willa Cather's life as does *My Ántonia*. Red Cloud appears again, this time as Black Hawk. William and Caroline Cather are present as Josiah and Emmaline Burden. The entire Miner family play the parts of the Harlings; Herbert Bates serves as the model for Gaston Cleric. Even secondary characters, such as Blind d'Arnault, the Negro pianist, or Wick Cutter, the degenerate money-lender, have their origins in people from Cather's past. The author herself is thinly disguised as James Quayle Burden, better known as Jim, and the description of his personality written into the introduction could easily be used as a definition of Willa Cather.

Jim Burden possessed a 'naturally romantic and ardent disposition', which, the author decided, 'made him seem very funny as a boy' — a reference to her own youthful eccentricities perhaps? It is precisely that ardent quality, however, that has been the secret of his success. 'He loves with a personal passion the great country through which his railway runs and branches', we are told, and even though he is now a mature middle-aged man, Jim is still able 'to lose himself in those big Western dreams'. He could be Willa Cather's twin, right down to his changeable blue eyes.

The most revealing phrase comes when the anonymous author makes a deal with Jim. It is agreed that they should each write down their impressions of Ántonia, a Bohemian girl they knew on the Divide, and the heroine of the novel. 'Of course', Jim replies ponderously, 'I should have to do it in a direct way, and say a good deal about myself. It's through myself that I knew and felt her. . . .'

And here we are left with an enigma. Willa Cather was to say in an interview that most of what she knew about Annie Sadilek, Ántonia's real-life counterpart, had come from the impressions of young men who knew her; Woodress adds that she wrote as much to Will Owen Jones, maintaining that, due to her experience of ghosting for S.S. McClure, she felt competent to write as from a first-person male character. Yet so many of Jim Burden's experiences are clearly her own, and the narration *is* direct, does reveal much about herself; one wonders whether Cather didn't use this male character as a shield for her private life — not necessarily in lesbian terms, but because prying eyes annoyed her in any case. The true extent to which Jim Burden is autobiographical will always be subject to speculation; there is no such problem, however, with Ántonia herself, the heroine of the novel.

Ántonia Shimerda, the Bohemian immigrant girl around whom the story revolves, was based upon a real-life friend of the Cather family, Annie Sadilek, whom Cather always tried to visit during her trips back to Red Cloud. Three years after *My Ántonia* was published, Willa Cather would declare that Annie was 'one of the truest artists I ever knew in the keenness and sensitiveness of her enjoyment, in her love of people and in her willingness to take pains'. In short, Annie was a natural artist, an unconscious embodiment of both land and woman, as strong and beautiful an image in herself as the famous plough against the sun. If Thea Kronborg emerged as vital because she had been endowed with Cather's own passion, how much more alive does Ántonia seem — she had, after all, been modelled upon a living being whom the author loved deeply. Because the story was one of feeling, Cather chose to construct it in the first person. The result of that emotional depth has frequently been called the finest of Cather's novels.

In telling the story, the author discarded the excessive detail she had used in *The Song of the Lark* (between Fremstad's magnetism and her own emotional/mnemonic outpourings, Cather had been unable to resist the urge to tell everything). With the character of Annie Sadilek, she returned to the process of simplification and began to act upon the principles of writing which were eventually set down in 'The Novel Démeublé', her essay on the 'unfurnished' novel. 'The higher processes of art', she declared, 'are all processes of simplification. The novelist must learn to write, and then he must unlearn it. . . .' And to be sure, *My Ántonia* is beautiful in and because of its simplicity.

Five sections trace the life of Ántonia Shimerda through the

Plates 1 and 2. Cather's paternal grandparents William and Caroline Cather

3. Cather's birthplace — Grandmother Boak's house, Back Creek, Virginia

4. Cather's childhood home at Red Cloud, Nebraska

Plates 5 and 6. Cather's parents Charles and Virginia Cather

Plates 7 and 8. The transformation from Willa as a conventionally pretty girl aged ten to a mannish adolescent with cropped hair and boy's clothes

9. Cather in about 1905, showing an uncharacteristic interest in dress

10. Prairie landscape in Webster Country, Nebraska

eyes of Jim Burden: as a child enduring the harsh life of the Divide; as a hired girl at the Miners' in Black Hawk; as the young woman Jim leaves behind when he goes away to college (away from him, Ántonia goes on to her fate of pregnancy and abandonment by an unscrupulous railroadman); finally, some twenty years later, Jim returns to the Divide to find that Ántonia has come into her own at last. In direct contrast to his own unhappy union, she is married and radiant, the wife of a good-hearted, unambitious Bohemian (Anton Cuzak) and the mother of a swarm of beautiful children. The children are her crowning glory; all will grow up unashamed of their native tongue, and all will adhere to the old-fashioned values and manners that were so dear to Willa Cather's heart. They are Ántonia's legacy: hope for the future, carrying within themselves the traditions of the past.

Though haggard and worn by the end of the novel, Ántonia is none the less Cather's greatest triumphant persona, the embodiment of all that is good in life and love, a natural Madonna of the Plains, a shining symbol of the art of life. Years before, when Jim was about to leave for college, he, Ántonia, and two other 'hired girls' (the term grated upon Isabelle's Eastern sensibilities) had gone on a farewell picnic beside the river on the edge of town. As the sun began to set, they witnessed the following scene — surely one of the most-quoted passages of American literature:

> Just as the lower edge of the red disk rested on the high fields against the horizon, a great black figure suddenly appeared. . . . In a moment we realized what it was. On some upland farm, a plough had been left standing in the field. The sun was sinking just behind it. Magnified across the distance by the horizontal light, it stood out against the sun, was exactly contained within the circle of the disk; the handles, the tongue, the share — black against the molten red. There it was, heroic in size, a picture writing on the sun.

The greatness of the image lasts only for an instant; then it fails, absorbed once again into the vastness of the prairie. Although the vision may be taken to stand for a number of things — the enduring quality of man and the country, for example — the impression is most like Ántonia herself.

After seeing her as a triumphal figure in the midst of her family, Jim thinks that Ántonia had always been a woman to leave 'images in the mind that did not fade — that grew stronger with time'. His musing searches for the secret of her inner beauty: 'She still had that something which fires the imagination, could still stop one's breath for a moment by a look or gesture that somehow revealed a meaning in common things. . . . She was a rich mine of life, like the founders of early races.'

Alexandra Bergson comes to terms with the land, using her love and understanding strength to create a life out of the soil. Thea Kronborg reconciles herself to the passion of music. Both possess a singlemindedness of purpose, great love, and great imagination, and both achieve success at a price. While sharing their traits of love and strength, Ántonia Shimerda brings with her a subtle difference. She does not strive consciously towards an ideal; she simply lives and loves, loves everything: land, people, life itself. She reveals an ideal by her own existence, and though she, too, has suffered hardship — a father's suicide, a slave-driving brother, a lover's desertion — hers is the most complete triumph.

In one respect, Ántonia may almost be viewed as a synthesis of Alexandra and Thea. Alexandra is an extension of nature; Thea, an extension of the beauty of the creative impulse. Both join together in Ántonia who, with the strength of one and the sensitivity of the other, becomes a nearly perfect whole. There are, however, several characteristics which the three heroines have in common. All come from foreign stock; two of the three are immigrants and retain the use of their mother tongue and, while Thea was born in the New World, it is her Old-World Swedishness that sets her apart — one could never classify her as belonging to the 'Americans'. All are strong women, survivors, yet they manage to retain a high degree of sensitivity in a harsh environment; and all, of course, have come through hardship to triumph.

When the novels are viewed as a whole, they are suggestively autobiographical, indicating that Cather had been reliving her own past, coming to terms with it through writing her books. In the first, the land is the overpowering image, just as it was to Willa the child. Next, art comes to the fore and, through Thea, one can see Cather's own awakening to creative talent, and the subsequent struggles towards success; while the *Lark* was being written, she was experiencing her own 'debut' with *O Pioneers!* — much like Thea's arrival at the Met. Finally, these two lives are combined in Ántonia. By writing herself so vividly into the novel, Cather had come to terms with her own origins once and for all, discovering the great depth of her love not only for the land but also for the arts and for the intrinsic beauty of life and its natural, human and eternal manifestations in the beauty of 'common things'. She had come to realise that there was just as much 'art' contained in a large, loving Bohemian family in Nebraska as there was in the voice of a Wagnerian prima donna; Cather had caught up with herself, with her own present. It is no coincidence that Jim Burden's narrative ends with an account of his 're-visitation' to Ántonia after a long absence. A few years previously Cather herself had had just such an encounter with Annie Sadilek, now Pavelka. With *My Ántonia* she had finally arrived at the present. The only part of her own early life as yet unreconciled was her Virginian heritage, and that would take almost a lifetime to achieve.

Bridging the Present: One of Ours

Unfortunately, the most triumphant of Cather's novels fell victim to a triumph of larger proportions. *My Ántonia* appeared in 1918, just a few weeks before the end of the First World War, and this unfortunate timing, coupled with a weak promotional campaign and the book's drab cover, resulted in a poor reception. Despite high praise from critics such as Mencken, Randolph Browne and Houghton Mifflin's own Ferris Greenslet, the initial sales for *My Ántonia* were quite low (a situation that was to change dramatically over the next two decades). A general dissatisfaction caused Willa Cather to change her publishers and, from 1920 onwards, she took all her manuscripts to Alfred A. Knopf, a new young publisher whose Borzoi editions she already admired. The partnership continued for the rest of her life.

Meanwhile, other changes loomed ahead, blown in by the winds of war. During May 1918, G.P. Cather, the son of Willa's Aunt Franc, had been killed in the fighting round Cantigny in France. While visiting Red Cloud that summer, Willa Cather was able to read the letters her young cousin had written to his mother during his military service. The feelings, thoughts, indeed, the entire personality she found there were so moving that she resolved — for once consciously — to make her next novel a war story. The hero would be based on young G.P., 'just a red-headed prairie boy', she told a reporter, her own flesh and blood, and a Nebraskan. In the autumn she began work on the manuscript which eventually became *One of Ours*.

The plot is simple enough. It focuses upon Claude Wheeler, an awkward, serious youth, too sensitive for the coarse life of a modern Nebraska farm. His belief in taking pains and his respect for tradition place him in constant conflict with his crass, overbearing father and his materialistic brothers. Claude finds an ally of sorts in Mahailey, the simple, loyal mountain woman who works for the Wheelers, and also to a certain extent in his mother, Evangeline. The mother/son relationship is tender and close, but Evangeline believes that Claude's restlessness stems from the fact that he isn't 'saved', and doesn't have a God to follow. A short spell of education at the state university only makes matters worse, for this, too, is taken from him by Mr Wheeler, who leaves on a business venture with another son, placing Claude in charge of the farm during his absence.

Claude seeks solace in marriage, but it is an ill-fated match: the woman he chooses is frigid, a religious fanatic who finally disappears to China as a missionary. Finally, war breaks out, furnishing Claude with a cause he can believe in, as well as an escape from his slow death in Nebraska: he enlists and is sent to France, where he finds both companions and values he can admire. In the end Claude gives his life for that new-found country; he dies at peace with himself and with the world at last.

G.P. Cather was in fact only a pretext for the novel for, though genuinely fond of him, Willa Cather does not seem to have known her cousin at all well. *One of Ours* may have grown out of the memories and experiences of the author and of other personalities, but it was really the product of Cather's own disillusionment with the emerging American way of life as she perceived it. Throughout the war years, she had often seemed oblivious to the events that were changing the shape of the world. Yet all the time, during her return visits to Red Cloud, she had been observing the effect of those changes upon the society she had grown up in. Divided loyalties among the immigrant plains folk; shifting values; above all, the pre-war growth of a more materialistic society . . . Cather had seen and felt it all with her special sort of sympathy. Once the past had been dealt with finally through *My Ántonia*, these troublesome feelings demanded an outlet of their own. The death of her cousin provided that outlet, especially when she found glimpses of her own feelings in his letters. It is unlikely that Willa Cather would ever have been so cold-hearted as to use the death of a relative for her own purposes; probably she came to believe that she really *did* know that boy as well as herself (a statement she made to interviewers). Yet it cannot be denied that the character of Claude Wheeler is a figure more of her own creation than one drawn from life. Like Bartley Alexander before him, Claude serves as a channel for the author's feelings; he is much more than just a red-haired prairie boy.

Although he does not 'see pictures', as Cather would say, Claude none the less feels the need for a purpose, for an ideal. He needs a set of values that he can admire and serve, yet he does not know where or how to start searching for them. When he tries to explain his frustration with the everyday world to a Bohemian friend, he finds it impossible to put those feelings into words, for they are not defined in his own mind. 'What do you expect from life?' asks Ernest Havel, to which Claude replies: 'Well, if we've only got once to live, it seems like there ought to be something — well, something *splendid* about life, sometimes'.

The solution to his yearning does not lie in the Nebraska in which he lives. Gone are pioneer women such as Alexandra Bergson, who turned the plains into a kind of garden of values. Where Willa Cather had recently lauded the good in her prairie community, now she concentrated on its faults, and when she came down on them, she came down hard. 'With prosperity came a kind of callousness; everybody wanted to destroy the old things they used to take pride in. . . . It was less trouble to run into town in an automobile and buy fruit than it was to raise it. . . . Evidently it took more intelligence to spend money than to make it.' Even the farmers who had once worked together as friends were now at odds with each other, suing neighbours right and left.

Cather sends Claude to college to show him the 'right' way of living. In the Erlich family, modelled upon the Louis Westermanns of Cather's college days, Claude finds the sort of society he worships. His first impression is that they are rich — no doubt derived from the characteristic Wheeler way of thinking in which money is equated with happiness. Soon he realizes that they are not; they simply know how to live, 'spent their money on themselves, instead of on machines to do the work and machines to entertain people. Machines . . . could not make pleasure, whatever else they could do.' Claude had been denied real pleasure all his life; he is denied even the pleasures of the flesh, because of his wife's religious fanaticism. Willa Cather, who had herself renounced religion in her youth, was just beginning to grapple with feelings of spiritual uncertainty. In 1922, the year in which *One of Ours* was published, she joined the Episcopal Church, and faith began to play an increasingly important role in her life.

For Claude, however, religion is not the answer. He is neither talented enough to be an artist, nor zealous enough to be a priest, yet he possesses an artist's longing and a priest's love of sacrifice. Battle found him a willing victim: 'That was one of the things about this war. It took a little fellow from a little town, gave him an air and a swagger, a life like a movie-film — and then a death like the rebel angels.'

France became the ideal Claude would fight and die for; it became his adopted homeland. His response to France is the same response Willa Cather gave in 1902. Contrasting her perception of the French with the emerging trends in the USA (Cather had visited France again in 1919/20), the author used Claude to voice her worst fears about the course of life in America: 'There was no chance for the kind of life he wanted at home, where people were always buying and selling, building and pulling down. He had begun to believe that the Americans were a people of shallow emotions . . . if it was true, there was no cure for it.'

Besides giving him an ideal to live by and an adopted country, the war brings Claude the friendship denied him in his youth when he meets David Gerhardt, a talented musician. The character of Gerhardt is based on the violinist David Hochstein, another soldier who apparently found spiritual solace through the war, only to be killed in action in the same year as Cather's cousin. Hochstein's letters to his mother were quoted by Willa Cather in an interview with the *New York Herald* in 1922. 'Everyone finds his belief, his religion', Hochstein had written. 'Here I have found mine. I adhere to no creed, no more than my father did, . . . but dear mother, I *believe*. I have faith. I know that for all these heroic souls gone to the beyond there is some future. . . . You don't try to explain it — but you know it in France.' Cather said that she would have given a great deal to know what had so revolutionized Hochstein. Before the war he had been a questioning agnostic Socialist.

Although David Gerhardt and Claude Wheeler had been worlds apart in background, the war had given them a common ground of faith. The feeling is evident in the last few days of Claude's life, when he reflects upon the knowledge that war meant 'men could still die for an idea; and would burn all they had made to keep their dreams'. Both Claude and David Gerhardt die for those dreams.

The final scene in the novel returns to Nebraska, where Claude's mother reads his letters and mourns him, although it is a sadness tinged perhaps with relief; his letters had revealed a new, positive awareness in him, they glowed with his increasing happiness at finding both a cause and a reason for living. In some ways, Evangeline Wheeler considers, death came almost as a blessing.

He died believing his own country better than it is, and France better than any country can ever be. And those were beautiful beliefs to die with. Perhaps it was as well to see that vision, and then to see no more. She would have dreaded the awakening. . . . She feels as if God had saved him from some horrible suffering, some horrible end.

One of Ours signalled a further change in Willa Cather's writing. In one sense the book carried on the triumphal tradition of her three previous works for, although Claude perishes, he does so gloriously, believing he has served a higher cause. Unlike the last three novels, however, Cather steps back from Claude, revealing to the reader more of the truth surrounding those beliefs: in a sense they were false ideals and, had he lived, it is probable that Claude Wheeler may well have joined the ranks of postwar suicides. Once again death comes to the male hero, one whose searching has led him away from the right direction. Claude's pursuit was more valiant than Bartley Alexander's — it was not that his quest was selfish; merely that his ideals were too unrealistic. But in Cather's novels the American male always

103

loses out; even Godfrey St Peter of *The Professor's House*, though he survives physically, will die a spiritual death. Cather's own worst fears and frustrations often seemed to take on a male persona.

Yet Willa Cather was not alone in feeling disillusioned with the face of American 'progress' at the time. Immediately after the war the nation was fraught with uncertainty; Wilsonian idealism had been replaced by apathy. The only sure point was the businessman's prosperity, and as the dollar signs rose moral and cultural values plummeted. The intellectual migration to Paris began, and for those who stayed behind, among them H.L. Mencken and Sinclair Lewis, relentless criticism became the dominant note. In one sense, *One of Ours* reflected not only one writer's uncertainty, but the emerging mood of a new decade.

Though it won the Pulitzer Prize for Literature in 1923, *One of Ours* was not a great critical or popular success. Cather had once more dumbfounded her readers by changing her style as well as her material; she was roundly criticized as a woman trying to write about a man's war, and it is true that in the actual battle scenes, as well as in the portrayal of military life, she was out of her depth. The finest parts of the novel are the character portraits drawn from life: Mahailey, for example, based upon Margie Anderson, or Evangeline Wheeler, in whom traces of Aunt Franc may be seen. Although the criticism surrounding *One of Ours* annoyed her, Cather herself remained firm. She said that the story had taken a great deal out of her, and for years afterwards maintained that Claude was her own favourite of all her heroes. Elsewhere, in private correspondence, she conceded that she had been out of her depth; none the less, she had no regrets about attempting it.

'It was hard to cease to do the thing I do best', Cather admitted in an interview, 'but we all have to pay a price for everything we accomplish and because I was willing to pay so much to write about this boy I felt that I had a right to do so.'

Willa Cather must have cared deeply for her cousin, although she had not known him intimately. Yet it was his beliefs, or his *need* to believe — feelings which had coursed through her own veins — that caused the story to come to light. It was certainly not the lad himself.

During the four years that elapsed between the idea for *One of Ours* and its publication in 1922, life did not stand still. Following her decision to take her works to Knopf, it was agreed to bring out a collection of short stories, *Youth and the Bright Medusa*. Four of the tales had previously appeared in *The Troll Garden*: 'Paul's Case', 'A Wagner Matinee', 'A Death in the Desert' and 'The Sculptor's Funeral'. There were also four new stories, previously published in various magazines. In each of these, the focus is once more on art and artists, this time, however, with a difference: the creative passion takes second place, while the main themes concern the artists and their usually unhappy effect upon other people. Of the four — 'Coming, Aphrodite!', 'The Diamond Mine', 'A Golden Slipper' and 'Scandal' — three deal with female singers; the same character appears in two of them and in both cases the women fall prey to greedy Philistines in the form of relatives, husbands and music coaches. Successful as artists, failures in personal relationships . . . here was one of Cather's favourite themes, repeated yet again.

After *Youth* had been completed, Willa Cather and Edith Lewis travelled to Europe for a holiday as well as to gather material for *One of Ours*; at that time (1920) the book was only two-thirds complete. The women divided their time between Paris and Italy, and included a visit to Isabelle and Jan Hambourg, who guided Willa on a tour of the French devastation areas where she was able to find her cousin's grave. Relations between Cather and her former intimate were still somewhat strained; by this time she had grown to accept and even to like Jan, but the days of sanctuary she had experienced with Isabelle at the McClung residence were gone for ever. During the next year, when she had difficulty with the writing of *One of Ours*, Cather tried to solve the trouble by visiting Isabelle and Jan in Toronto, Canada, where they were living at the time. This arrangement proved reasonably satisfactory, yet it would never replace the sense of ease she had experienced working under Isabelle's protection in the house on Murray Hill.

It was while she was staying in Toronto that word reached Cather of the death of Lyra Anderson, the former wife of Governor Silas Garber of Red Cloud, and the town's one-time great lady. Cather was so disturbed by this news that she retired to bed. Within an hour she had received the outline of her next story, inspired by Mrs Garber. She travelled to Red Cloud after leaving the Hambourgs, and there can be little doubt that the memories conjured up by Mrs Garber's death, coupled with fresh impressions of her old home, left Cather's mind full of new material. At any rate, Edith Lewis recalled that in the spring before *One of Ours* was published, *A Lost Lady* was already begun.

Cycle of Defeat: the American/Lost Tales

In the collection of essays and prefaces entitled *Not Under Forty*, Willa Cather was to make her famous assertion that 'the world broke in two in 1922 or thereabouts' and she ranked herself with those belonging to the earlier side of that divide. Although she never exactly hid away from the modern age, there was no mistaking her disillusionment with the way the world was turning — that had been stated clearly enough in *One of Ours*. This new era, these Twenties; she found it impossible to take them seriously. Neither did she have patience with the 'lost generation' writers. How ironic then that the result of such dissatisfaction should produce her own lost generation of heroes and heroines, the first appearing in *A Lost Lady*.

'Thirty or forty years ago in one of those grey towns along the Burlington railroad, which are so much greyer today than they were then. . . .' Even in its opening lines the reader is brought face to face with Willa Cather's feelings about the modern age. The novel is divided into two main parts (reflecting the manner in which Cather had so recently divided the world), and in the early stages of part one, the reader's first response is that here is a story about an exceptional, lovely woman, one to be admired; in a certain sense she is admirable indeed. Marian Forrester is the second wife of Captain Daniel Forrester. Some twenty-five years younger than her husband, she is a beautiful dark-haired woman, kind-hearted, sociable, spontaneous, a woman who runs to meet arriving guests without pausing to fix her hair or to change from her dressing gown. Under her influence, the Forrester home has become a grand showplace for the town of Sweet Water (Red Cloud), with Mrs Forrester at its hub. Her qualities are revealed first through the eyes of a group of 12-year-old boys, principally Niel Herbert, who is infatuated with Marian for a number of years.

We next see Marian through Niel's eyes some seven years later.

A succession of droughts and crop failures have forced many of the farmers to leave the territory, and ill-fortune has also visited the Captain, who has suffered increasingly poor health following a riding accident. Marian Forrester, however, although no longer able to winter amid the sparkle of Denver society, makes the best of things by throwing lavish parties. To one such occasion she invites Niel, now a law student. Another man, a stranger, is also present, and Niel senses an evil aura about him. In the following weeks, the truth is slowly revealed about Marian Forrester: devoted in one sense to her older husband, the two have never truly been compatible and, frustrated, Marian has been having an affair with Frank Ellinger, the stranger. It is not until the following spring, however, that Niel makes this discovery, and feels the sharp pain of seeing an idol shattered.

Captain Forrester's bank in Denver fails, and when he goes away on business, Ellinger takes the opportunity to return to Marian. Sensing impropriety but still blind to the truth, Niel rises early one morning to leave a bouquet of flowers on Marian Forrester's window sill. The depiction of his moment of realization is poignant, filled with pain and rage, and represents Willa Cather at her finest:

> There was an almost religious purity about the fresh morning air. . . . He would make a bouquet for a lovely lady; a bouquet gathered off the cheeks of morning . . . These roses, only half awake, in the defencelessness of utter beauty. . . . As he bent to place the flowers on the sill, he heard from within a woman's soft laughter; impatient, indulgent, teasing, eager. Then another laugh, very different, a man's. And it was fat and lazy, — ended in something like a yawn.

Enraged and ashamed, Niel flings the bouquet into the mud and storms away with his broken dreams.

'Whatever is felt upon the page without being specifically named there', Willa Cather stated in 'The Novel Démeublé', 'that, one might say, is created. It is the inexplicable presence of the thing not named, . . . that gives high quality to the novel.' Surely the evocation of the unnamed scene behind Marian Forrester's window is creative writing of the highest quality.

It is from this point, especially after Captain Forrester becomes even more immobile after a stroke, that Marian Forrester's character declines. When Niel returns to visit Sweet Water two years later, he discovers that she has entrusted what little money there is left to Ivy Peters, a man noted for unscrupulous dealing, already introduced at the beginning of the novel as a cruel youth, spoiling the younger boys' picnic by torturing a bird. With the Captain immobilized, Peters has the run of the land and Mrs Forrester is at his mercy. Her former lover, Ellinger, has left her and married. When Captain Forrester finally dies, Marian experiences some kind of breakdown, even taking Ivy into her bed to ensure her survival. When Niel eventually returns to Boston, he is both depressed and disgusted, convinced that he has witnessed the passing of a golden age.

> He had seen the end of an era, the sunset of the pioneer. He had come up on it when already its glory was nearly spent. . . . It was what he most held against Mrs Forrester; that she was not willing to immolate herself, like the widow of all these great men, and die with the pioneer period to which she belonged; that she preferred life on any terms.

These are Cather's sentiments, the same that she had worked out for Claude: a glorious death is infinitely preferable to a life spent at odds with one's time. Yet despite Niel's disenchantment, Marian Forrester remains in his mind through the years as a charming memory; Cather's love for and understanding of her character allows no less for her. When Niel hears of his lost lady's remarriage to a rich Englishman and then of her subsequent death, he feels a sad relief: at least she had been cared for to the end.

After the shock caused by *One of Ours*, this short novel, written in less than a quarter of the time taken for the earlier work, became an immediate, enthusiastic success. When it appeared in 1923, *A Lost Lady* became 'the toast', as Elizabeth Sergeant put it. Most critics were delighted with the book, though some did miss the point (Somerset Maugham, for example, saw it as the story of Niel's disenchantment). Warner Brothers bought the film rights, and when the film was first shown in Red Cloud in 1925, nearly everyone thought it an accurate, well-presented portrayal of the Garbers — everyone, that is, except the author. She immediately forbade the dramatisation of any of her other works — presumably finding screen exposure, with its inevitable misinterpretations, upsetting, an invasion of privacy. *A Lost Lady* was formed from her personal memories of Lyra Garber; the film version seemed an unbearable travesty.

In the coming years, Willa Cather became obsessed with the idea of protecting her copyrights and that paranoia expanded to include her personal life as well. When Elizabeth Sergeant proposed writing a short article on her friend (a piece later published in Sergeant's *Fire Under the Andes*), Cather's cool reception of the idea was a warning not to delve too deeply. Afterwards, indeed, the friendship was never quite so free and open as it had been. Many previous biographers have made much of such instances, which contribute to the portrait of Willa Cather, Recluse. This was not strictly the case. To be sure, she had an obsessive dislike of all forms of noise and interruptions, going so far as to rent the apartment above her own to preempt footsteps overhead. She had her Friday afternoon At Homes, when visitors were free to call; otherwise, it was generally known that Miss Cather was not to be disturbed. Yet seclusion is necessary for many artists, and Cather's actions — disconnecting the phone, dodging reporters — were still not as extreme as they might have been. Willa Cather was 'never a recluse by nature', Edith Lewis wrote: 'She loved people, and had a warm, eager, impulsive interest in all kinds of people. . . . It was the completeness of her response to people that made ordinary human contacts more taxing for her than most. . . . The luxury she prized above all others was freedom; and she now found her freedom hampered at every turn.'

Freedom not just to create, but to be; freedom in which to think and to feel. For Willa Cather such freedom came to mean solitude, but generally it was a solitude both shared and nurtured by devoted companions: first with Isabelle and later with Edith Lewis. Once the McClung house had been taken from her, Cather discovered other private creative places.

The first was the Shattuck Inn in Jaffrey, New Hampshire, where she had visited Isabelle and Jan Hambourg during 1917. After they left, Cather stayed on to write parts of *My Ántonia*, and thereafter would return to the Inn nearly every year for peace and solitude and long woodland walks. Another haven was discovered at Grand Manan Island, New Brunswick, during 1922. She and Edith Lewis first rented a house there and then later built a primitive cottage which provided them with a retreat until the Second World War. Amid the natural beauty of this cool, green craggy island, 'there was solitude without loneliness', Edith Lewis recalled. Of course, the Bank Street apartment was always a good place in which to work, but it was not surrounded by the nature that Willa Cather loved so much.

Perhaps another reason for her solitary retreats may be found in the ill health which had begun to plague her during this period. Cather detested being ill, and would never have wanted herself exposed to visitors with even the slightest of disabilities. Although normally very strong, she had over the years experienced several setbacks of various kinds: blood poisoning in 1914 while writing *The Song of the Lark*; occasional bouts of influenza; tonsillitis during the winter of 1921/2. The most annoying complaint occurred during 1923 while she and Edith Lewis were in France. Neuritis so inflamed her right arm and shoulder that she couldn't write for some time, and the spring and summer were left barren. It was November before Cather was able to begin her next project within the familiar surroundings of Bank Street.

She was by now a month short of her fiftieth birthday, an age which seems for her to have been one of retrospection. Her reputation as a novelist was firmly established, yet, as she had expected, success had come with a price — it was much more difficult to keep her treasured solitude these days. Age, always an enemy, had also begun to creep in; illness reminded her of that. She could not feel at home in the postwar era and its new generation. Even New York was changing, becoming more hectic both for work and leisure. As Hartley Grattan put it, the 'Big Apple' exhibited a 'distinct tendency to live in the headlines of life'. Cather felt out of touch with those headlines; feeling rather as though life were moving on without her, she stepped back for an analysis and a summing up. The result was the novel that James Woodress so aptly calls a 'spiritual autobiography', *The Professor's House* (1925). Edith Lewis would have agreed; it was, she thought, the most personal of Cather's novels. In a copy she autographed to the poet Robert Frost, Cather herself called it a story of 'letting go with the heart'.

Godfrey St Peter, the novel's hero, has a similar upbringing and background to his creator. Born on a farm near the lush country around Lake Michigan, he too was 'dragged' when young to the barren wheat fields of Kansas, where he 'nearly died of it'. Now he has returned to the country of his childhood, having taken a post as professor in a nearby college, chosen partly, we are told, for its proximity to the lake. After several years' teaching he produces his great work: an eight-volume epic, *Spanish Adventurers in North America*, which at first creates no stir, but then wins him a substantial history award and world-wide acclaim. At the time that the novel opens, the long project is complete and Godfrey feels exhausted and at a loss; there is a 'diminution of ardour' for which he can find no explanation. Close to his creator's own age, Professor St Peter feels thoroughly out of place in the new era. The postwar decline in moral standards; a fascination with and inclination towards mass-produced goods; the influx of scientific gadgets . . . these are factors which he sees as conspiring against the old values of beauty, passion and ideals. As St Peter tells his students, he does not think much of science as a part of progress:

It hasn't given us any richer pleasures, as the Renaissance did, nor any new sins — not one! Indeed, it takes our old ones away. It's the laboratory, not the Lamb of God, that taketh away the sins of the world. You'll agree there is not much thrill about a physiological sin . . . I don't think you help people by making their conduct of no importance — you impoverish them. . . . Art and religion (they are the same thing in the end, of course) have given man the only happiness he has ever had.

The professor's feeling of being out of place has affected him not only emotionally, but physically as well; fatigue haunts him and makes him nostalgic. As he looks back over his life, he does not regret it, but it seems far removed from the person that he is now.

When the book opens, another change is about to occur in Professor St Peter's life. His wife to whom he has been married for many years, and for whom he now feels no particular affection, has had a modern house built for them, befitting his new success. Ugly and inconvenient though his old house is, the professor is reluctant to give it up; for him it represents twenty years of happy life, work and emotions; it contains his cluttered attic study. Just like Cather's Rose Bower, or the attic at the McClung's, this room is 'the one place in the house where he could get isolation, insulation from the engaging drama of domestic life'. It, too, is old-fashioned and inconvenient, sporting a kerosene lamp and a faulty stove (which almost proves to be the death of him). Through the room's one square window, however, St Peter can just see the blue waters of Lake Michigan, the symbol of his childhood and of his youth and desire. Because he cannot bear the thought of losing this refuge, the professor rents the whole of the house after all else has been moved away, simply for the use of the attic study — just as Cather had rented an entire apartment for the sake of silence.

It is not only change or the modern world from which Professor St Peter flees; he feels constantly alienated from his own family, in particular his wife, Lillian. Of his two daughters, Rosamund and Kathleen, he possesses some rapport with the latter, but finds Rosamund grown uncompromisingly materialistic. Her husband, Louie Marsellus, has unwittingly corrupted her with money; it is generally surmised that Marsellus, as a well-meaning but exasperating Jewish son-in-law, is modelled upon Jan Hambourg. Though St Peter has more in common with his other son-in-law, who at least shares his own pleasure in swimming, the petty quarrels inherent within the family circle drive him deeper into himself. When Marsellus proposes a visit to France for his parents-in-law, St Peter declines: 'It's not wholly a matter of the calendar', he says. 'It's the feeling that I've put a great deal behind me, where I can't go back to it again — and I don't really wish to go back.' A previous passage is even more revealing: 'There were some advantages about being a writer of histories. The desk was a shelter one could hide behind, it was a hole one could creep into.' While his family is away, the professor uses his solitude to relive the brightest spot of his recent past, his encounter with the young Tom Outland.

Outland (and surely the name is symbolic) had come into St Peter's orbit several years earlier as a raw prairie boy, an orphan, but with a special quality that the professional side of St Peter recognised. The two men became fast friends; Outland made remarkable progress with his studies. His discovery of a unique and valuable scientific method was to bring him financial security and he became engaged to Rosamund St Peter. Tragically, he was killed in the First World War. Ironically, it was his discovery, patented and exploited by Louie Marcellus, that laid the foundation of Rosamund and Louie Marcellus's fortune and was thus, unwittingly, the cause of her material corruption.

Before his meeting with Godfrey, however, Tom Outland lived a different sort of life, one in which he discovered the Blue Mesa and its cliff dwellings (based undoubtedly on Dick Wetherill's experiences, which he had related to Cather in 1912). When Tom tried to publicise his finds, he found that the 'museum people' in Washington, DC, were simply not interested — they, like everyone else, had been corrupted by the pressures of modern life, and were interested only in free lunches and advancing their own positions. In the meantime, Tom's friend, Ruddy Blake, had misguidedly sold all the artefacts. A rift between the two followed, leaving Outland to travel east to gain an education.

The section devoted to Tom Outland provides a story within a story, a small open window to let the fresh Blue Mesa air into Professor St Peter's cluttered and oppressive life — exactly the effect Cather had said she wanted to achieve by inserting the *nouvelle* into the *roman* (*On Writing*, pages 31–2).

In Book III of *The Professor's House* attention is again focused on Professor St Peter himself, now more introspective than ever. With Tom Outland he had found a second youth; now, however, he feels as if he has come to the end of his life, as, in one sense, he has. His days pass in state of blissful apathy, coupled with a morbid acceptance of death, which appears to him as the final, peaceful house. Shortly after receiving word of his family's impending return, St Peter lights the little gas stove in his study one night; the light blows out and he is nearly asphyxiated. Death is not to be wooed so easily, however: Augusta, the sewing woman, finds him and pulls him out in time. When he regains consciousness, St Peter knows that he has 'let something go — and it was gone: something very precious, that he could not consciously have relinquished, probably'. The 'something' is his youth and his passion, the strength to pursue the ideals that make life worth living. The closing passages of the book are particularly poignant:

He had never learned to live without delight. And he would have to learn to, just as, in a Prohibition country, he supposed he would have to learn to live without sherry. Theoretically he knew that life is possible, may even be pleasant, without joy, without passionate griefs. But it had never occurred to him that he might have to live like that.

Because the professor is willing to live life without joy, instead of opting for death, he is linked to Marian Forrester: both have outlived their times, both have abandoned the strength of their beliefs; hence both are lost. In this novel of 'letting go', what was it that the author herself relinquished? The answer, I think, is youth; Cather had finally to realise that the passion of her younger days was gone forever.

Defeatist and depressing *The Professor's House* may be, but it is as nothing compared to the final book in Cather's cycle of loss. *My Mortal Enemy* (1926) is more novella than novel — 18,000 words or so, and the epitome of the 'novel démeublé', for it is stripped of all description. Yet this short book is the most frighteningly bitter of all Cather's works, a psychological portrait of downfall through greed. It is also the book which reveals the least information about Cather's life. One slight clue may lie in a passing reference made by E.K. Brown in his biography of the novelist, to the effect that the protagonist was based upon a woman Cather knew 'through connections in Lincoln' and who died before the First World War.

This anonymous figure takes form as Myra Driscoll Henshawe, the events of whose life are seen through the eyes of Nellie Birdseye, one of Cather's few female narrators. Nellie is fifteen when the story opens. Our first glimpse of Myra shows us a short, plump woman in her mid-forties, still charming, still attractive in spite of her tendency to roundness and to double chins. Like Marian Forrester, she has an enchanting voice and engaging laughter yet, curiously, it is a voice that carries an undercurrent of menace. Again like Niel's Lost Lady, Myra's colourful life — which includes a break with her uncle, a lost inheritance and an elopement — has made her legendary in the small Illinois town from which she came.

Her husband Oswald, a Protestant, and the man with whom she, a Catholic, eloped, is of a gentler nature, less dynamic than his wife, and amiable. Nellie encounters them both for the first time at a party; she thinks that Oswald should have been a soldier, perhaps, or an explorer — instead, he has a dull office job which he endures in order to keep Myra in style. The two are genuinely in love at the beginning of the story, but there are early hints of Myra's grasping nature and extravagances that signal trouble later on.

Nellie and her Aunt Lydia spend Christmas with the Henshawes in New York, and through Nellie's impressions, we can glimpse the city as Willa Cather fell in love with it in 1904. New York is seen as a metropolis surrounded by 'good manners and courtesy, — like an open-air drawing-room'. There is an air of dignity and refinement; even the shrubs in the parks add to the pleasantly sociable feeling. The interiors of the Madison Square brownstones reflect the same elegant lifestyle: large, solid rooms, high ceilings, fireplaces, velvet curtains. Here Myra is in her element; she sends elegant and expensive gifts to her friend Modjeska, spends evenings at the opera and cultivates the company of artists of all sorts for her own satisfaction, while seeking out the 'moneyed people' for Oswald's business — a task she really dislikes but sees as necessary for their style of living. Beneath the charm, however, there lies an irrational greed. 'It's very nasty, being poor!' Myra exclaims. Although she is, in fact, rather well off she is never satisfied.

To Nellie, Myra is an enigma for, beneath her selfish exterior the older woman does genuinely care for people, feeling true distress when anything occurs to mar a friendship. Yet Myra remains a slave to her emotions and when she is angry, her feeling is frightening in its intensity. When husband and wife quarrel, Nellie watches as Myra's mouth, which can be so tender and loving, is contorted with emotion. 'Letting herself think harm of anyone she loved', Nellie remembered 'seemed to change her nature, even her features.' Similar remarks were made about Willa Cather in her time. The first part of the story ends upon this malevolent undertone

Part II opens ten years later, on a very different scene. Nellie, now twenty-five, has gone to a sprawling West Coast city in order to teach. By coincidence she moves into the same run-down apartment block where the Henshawes, with whom she lost touch years before, also live. Time has been hard on them; they live in real poverty and Myra, fatally ill, is slowly wasting away towards death. But even illness hasn't changed her indomitable spirit.

Nellie is pleased to find her 'strong and broken, generous and tyrannical, a witty and rather wicked old woman who hated life for its defeats, and loved it for its absurdities'. Though she seems bitter and broken, Myra is actually far less changed than Oswald, who now seems much older than his years. The rest of the novel deals with Myra's slow demise and her various soliloquies. Marriage, she thinks, has been the destruction of both parties — she should have chosen her uncle's inheritance rather than her love for Oswald. 'Money is a protection, a cloak', she says when disturbed by the sounds of neighbours overhead. 'It can buy one quiet, and some sort of dignity.' She is nothing if not honest: 'I am a greedy, selfish, worldly woman; I wanted success and a place in the world.'

Towards the end, Myra shows Nellie a bag of money that she has kept hidden in order to pay for masses for Modjeska (long since dead) and for herself, instead of using it to ease the burden of the present. She has at least made her peace with God, but even in her few final days she continues to lash out at Oswald, whom she loves but cannot stop hurting. It is a trait she admits to Nellie but insists upon justifying: 'People can be lovers and enemies at the same time, you know . . . . In age we lose everything, even the power to love.' It is just this love/hate relationship that is revealed in her haunting cry: 'Why must I die like this, alone with my mortal enemy?' Eventually she escapes, travelling to a headland overlooking the sea where she dies, watching the sunrise.

My Mortal Enemy seems a strange story to come from the author of *My Ántonia*, yet the reader should bear in mind that Cather was still upset and disillusioned during this period, feeling herself caught up in an age with which she had little sympathy. She had also been beset by illness: she had been in and out of hospitals with bouts of influenza, and was continually troubled by her neuritis. For a person who detested disability as much as Willa Cather, such physical setbacks must have led her to increased introspection. Perhaps in Myra Henshawe, Cather created an image of herself as she could have been without a creative outlet. Certainly there are similarities: Myra's strong emotions, so quickly reflected in her face; the passionate feelings of her youth; her paranoia about noise; her dislike of the onslaught of age; even her dislike of modern writers contrasted with her feeling for

Whitman. Indeed, it seems that Cather appears in several different persona at the same time; first as Nellie Birdseye, whose reaction to New York was Cather's own. Similarly, when Nellie becomes a teacher, it is as a compromise until she can find her true occupation. When Myra asks why she doesn't take up journalism, Nellie replies: 'Because I hate journalism. I know what I want to do, and I'll work my way out yet, if you'll only give me time.' These words could easily have been spoken by the Cather of the Pittsburgh years.

Finally, the author appears in the vignette of a young journalist, a companion of Oswald's. The description needs no introduction:

> She was perhaps eighteen, overgrown and awkward, with short hair and a rather heavy face; but there was something unusual about her clear, honest eye that made one wonder. She was always on the watch to catch a moment with Oswald, to get him to talk to her about music, or German poetry, or about the actors and writers he had known.

Whatever lies behind the creation of Myra Henshawe, it is she, more than Professor St Peter or Marian Forrester, who represents what Cather sees as the corruption of the modern age; she is her creator's most extreme, most desperate character. Unlike Cather's triumphant heroines, the three protagonists of the novels of loss have displaced themselves in society through their searching: Marian Forrester in her quest for society, sexuality and riches; Professor St Peter in his search for the renewal of youth; and Myra Henshawe in her greed for wealth and power. These three are all Americans, unlike the previous immigrant heroines with their Scandinavian backgrounds.

Cather deeply resented the passing of her youth and the loss of her time of greatest creative passion, when she was at ease with the society in which she lived — a society cut off for ever by the First World War. As a result, she had become embittered towards her contemporary 'Americans', and was increasingly critical of them. Claude Wheeler may have been inarticulate and awkward, but he gave his life for France, his adopted country; by doing so he was set just that bit higher than his countrymen. These others were survivors, compromising themselves and their values for the sake of mere existence — nothing could be less Catherian. She had written about them in order to purge herself of her feelings of hate. With the death of Myra Henshawe, the last and most bitter emotion left her. If she was unable to set her novels in the present, then Willa Cather would set them elsewhere, in the past that meant so much to her. This time, however, it would be a past rooted in faith.

7 Return to Full Circle

> To fulfil the dreams of one's youth; that is the best
> that can happen to a man. No worldly success can
> take the place of that.
>
> Father Vaillant to Archbishop Latour,
> *Death Comes for the Archbishop*

The sole passion of her youth had been to pursue and perfect her art; by the time *My Mortal Enemy* had been completed, Willa Cather had achieved her aspiration — to a greater or lesser degree — time and time again. Her standards never wavered; she never clung to one method of writing for the sake of satisfying her public. Like her best heroines, Cather was always searching for something higher; she experimented constantly, refined, simplified — a process that inspired awe among her admirers but exasperated her critics.

They never knew what to expect next from Cather; indeed, they had trouble classifying her existing work. For her part, the writer was no help at all, for she seldom discussed her writing. By now she had grown used to the critics' complaints, which she largely ignored. Critical discussion was redundant, unimportant. 'Anyone', she told Louise Bogan in 1931, 'who ever has experienced the delight of living with people and in places which are beautiful and which he loves, throughout the long months required to get them down on paper, would never waste a minute conjuring up lists of rules or tracing down reasons why.' Writing mattered. Explanations did not.

In spite of her reticence, such single-mindedness of purpose eventually brought the world to her door, and the 1920s found Willa Cather not a little surprised and bewildered at her own celebrity status. Her works had been translated into several languages; on both sides of the Atlantic she had most definitely 'arrived'. In 1922 a British opinion poll placed her among the six most important contemporary American writers. In 1925 and 1926 her name could be found next to Frost, Dreiser, E.A. Robinson, Wharton and Hergesheimer in the *London Mercury*. In

America she was ranked as the fourth leading writer in the nation for the decade ending in 1922; in 1929 she was at the top of that list.

Financial success followed such universal acclaim — a rather difficult adjustment to make. Profits from *A Lost Lady* helped to build the cottage on Grand Manan; *The Professor's House* added a mink coat to her wardrobe — a rare acquiescense to luxury. Mostly, however, Cather's earnings simply afforded her the security of a continued comfortable existence, and allowed her to spend money upon people she loved — by sending gift boxes to needy friends in Nebraska, for example, or paying the college fees of a younger relative. More enjoyable even than this, perhaps, her new financial stability gave her the freedom to travel. There had been a trip to France in 1923, for example, when she had visited the Hambourgs, travelled around, and had her portrait painted by Leon Bakst (it was not a success). That was not an entirely happy time, however, marred as it was by recurrent illness and mid-life crisis.

But now the bitterness expressed in *My Mortal Enemy* was a thing of the past and Willa Cather was ready to travel again. Once more she turned her face to the Southwest. In the summer of 1925 she and Edith Lewis journeyed to New Mexico, where they met Mabel Dodge Luhan in Santa Fe. Mrs Luhan offered the two women the use of a guest house in Taos. They stayed for two weeks, during which time Mabel's husband Tony, an Indian, took them for short drives in the surrounding countryside. Though by nature a reticent man, Tony none the less provided Willa Cather with a great deal of information about the land and the Indians; he seems to have been the prototype for Eusabio, the Navajo Indian in *Death Comes for the Archbishop*.

It was in Santa Fe, however, that Cather experienced another of her inner 'explosions' of inspiration. One night at the hotel she chose as her bedtime reading an obscure volume, *The Life of the Right Reverend Joseph P. Macheboeuf*, by one Father William Howlett. Macheboeuf had been vicar to Archbishop Lamy, the first Bishop of New Mexico; a statue of Lamy stood in front of Santa Fe Cathedral, and Cather had been interested in finding out more about the pioneer churchman. As she read Howlett's book late into the night, something about the life, work and relationship of Macheboeuf and Lamy touched a chord. 'There, in a single evening', Edith Lewis recalled, 'the idea of *Death Comes for the Archbishop* came to her, essentially as she afterwards wrote it.' The novel, an account of two French Catholic priests in the old Southwest, was to capture the imaginations of readers the world over. Critics hailed it as a masterpiece, on a par with *My Ántonia*; some even said that it was the best thing Cather had ever done — and she agreed with them.

The Novels of Faith

Death Comes for the Archbishop was one of the few works Cather chose to discuss of her own accord. Because of the enormous public response when the book was first published in 1927, she wrote her own account of its genesis in an open letter to the *Commonweal*.

The history of the Catholic Church in the Southwest had apparently intrigued her for many years, especially since her first visit to the territory in 1912. There in Santa Cruz, New Mexico, she had made the acquaintance of a priest, a Belgian named Father Haltermann, who had delighted in telling her about the country and the Indians of his eighteen missions. Even in the harsh and arid climate, the priest managed to keep a part of his own civilization around him, raising his own poultry and sheep and cultivating a marvellous vegetable and flower garden.

It was the actual church buildings themselves, however, that held a special fascination for Cather. Even the old, abandoned churches, with their wooden carvings and unusual frescoes seemed to be 'a direct expression of some very real and lively human feeling'. As she returned to the territory again and again, the history of these churches continued to attract her, but there were always other projects claiming her attention and, besides, she was not a Catholic — surely it was not her place to attempt such a novel.

Then came the trip of 1925, the statue of Archbishop Lamy and the book about Macheboeuf, which included in its text the letters Macheboeuf had written to his sister in France. The brotherly relationship between the two priests, their great faith and their dedication came alive for Willa Cather, a woman still struggling with her own beliefs. When she returned East that autumn, she made for Jaffrey and began to write, continuing to work on the book throughout the winter at Bank Street. The following summer found her back in New Mexico, verifying facts and obtaining fresh impressions: Ácoma, the Mesa Encantada, the villages of Isleta and Arroyo Hondo. By the autumn of 1926 she had completed what must be one of the most serenely beautiful books ever written, one which led Rebecca West to call her 'the most sensuous of writers'.

It is an extremely difficult book to describe, for *Death Comes for the Archbishop* comes to one as a whole, unique; an entity in its own right. In an essay on Katherine Mansfield, Willa Cather later wrote that 'the qualities of a second-rate writer can easily be defined, but a first-rate writer can only be experienced'. Such was the case with the *Archbishop*: no one denied its intrinsic beauty but it was almost impossible to classify. Most critics would not call it a 'novel', but could not find another category to which it plainly belonged; Cather herself preferred to call it a narrative. Classification, however, was only a minor consideration.

In simple terms, *Death Comes for the Archbishop* is a retelling based on the events recorded in Father Howlett's biography and supplemented by Cather's own experiences and those of her father. 'The writing', she said in her *Commonweal* letter, 'took only a few months because the book had all been lived many times before it was written.' In the book Lamy and Marcheboeuf have become Father Jean Marie Latour and Father Joseph 'Blanchet' Vaillant. A Prologue sets the beginning of the story in 1848, in Rome, and four churchmen are searching for a new vicar to send to the New World. The candidate, they are told, must be a young man of intelligence, strength, and above all, order, for the country is unforgiving. 'That country will drink up his youth and strength as it does the rain. He will be called upon for every sacrifice, quite possibly for martyrdom.' The candidate chosen is Jean Marie Latour.

Nine Books chart the struggles of Father Latour and his beloved friend Father Vaillant to nurture and build a faith amongst the primitive people of the Southwest. The priests share the qualities of Alexandra Bergson, for they, too, are pioneers in the wilderness, trying to create a dream from a harsh environment. Yet here the ideal they strive for is not Alexandra's harmony with the land, or Thea Kronborg's singing; neither is it the

122

feelings of life and love embodied in Ántonia — though she is, perhaps, the closest to them of the three. Here the dream takes the shape of faith, perhaps not so different an ideal after all, for Cather had come to believe that religion and art sprang from the same source. The major change that separates *Death Comes for the Archbishop* from the earlier novels is Cather's new method of construction.

'Since I first saw the Puvis de Chavannes frescoes of the life of Saint Genevieve', Cather explained, 'I have wished that I could try something a little like that in prose; something without accent, with none of the artificial elements of composition.' In essence, she wished to try the style of legend, in which great and little events occur side by side and are given equal prominence. Thus, *Death Comes for the Archbishop* unfolds naturally and simply. It gives the impression of unfolding before one, at the same time flowing outwards in all directions so that the reader, although aware of a chronological framework, is also given the total picture, the total 'fresco'.

Cather found a related technique in another source, a book published as *The Golden Legend*, a translation of a medieval manuscript composed of the lives of saints. In such accounts, trivial happenings are given as much prominence as more dramatic scenes. Thus in *Death Comes for the Archbishop*, Book II opens with the amusing tale of how Father Vaillant wheedles two mules out of a wealthy parishioner; the same mules then take the two priests into danger, when they arrive at the house of a homicidal American. In Book I, Father Latour's miraculous rescue in the desert is followed by a quiet scene: the two priests share a Christmas dinner.

Cather's elevation of 'the little' is evinced in that same scene, when Latour discourses on the importance of the smallest traditions. For a Christmas treat, Father Vaillant has meticulously prepared an onion soup in the French manner, and Latour seizes this opportunity to make his point. The soup, he says, is 'the result of a constantly refined tradition. There are nearly a thousand years of history in this soup.' Cather is present in this line; her own insistence upon the civilised, traditional manner of performing even small tasks is well-documented: 'She insisted upon the tarragon', Elizabeth Sergeant recalled, telling how Cather prepared her own French salad dressing. By her careful balancing of emphasis, Cather is able to create a panorama of events; she also places the reader in a god-like position: suddenly omnipresent, one is a witness to all the affairs — both large and small — of the priests' lives. Elizabeth Sergeant has called the book 'almost a miracle . . . like watching the emergence of the lunar moth from the chrysalis. The process and the creature are one and whole. . . .' Indeed, the book has the feeling of a beautiful tapestry which takes as its background the grandeur of the Southwest. Because of the continuous interplay between micro- and macrocosm the land itself is given universal status: the entire world assumes a totality in Latour's mind as he ponders his surroundings. Everything becomes a reflection of God: 'In all his travels, the Bishop had seen no country like this. From the flat red sea of sand rose great rock mesas, generally Gothic in outline, resembling vast cathedrals. . . .' And as he passes by the Mesa Encantada, Latour puzzles over the Indian tendency to build villages upon the mesas' almost inaccessible heights, and arrives once again at a cosmic solution: 'The rock, when one came to think of it, was the utmost expression of human need; even mere feeling yearned for it; it was the highest comparison of loyalty in love and friendship.'

Just as the trivial and the grandiose are placed side by side, so too are the other opposites of life: youth and old age; good and evil; rich and poor. Even the two priests, from the same seminary, are quite different. On the one hand is Latour: thoughtful, quiet, introspective. He is a man of refined tastes who finds it easier to relate to abstractions than to his human charges. Vaillant, on the other hand, is an energetic extrovert: his motto is 'rest in action', and his great energy sends him travelling throughout the country, sleeping in the humblest abodes. Physically ugly, he is the man of the people, the one to whom they respond. Because the novel contains within itself such opposing aspects of life, the reader can appreciate the care with which the author chose the title from the *Dance of Death*, Holbein's great cycle of engravings, in which death, a grinning skeleton, appears to fetch all to the same end.

It is at this point that there appears to have been a change in Cather's perceptions. When, at the end of the book, death finally draws near to Father Latour, now Archbishop, it is neither as Myra Henshawe's dreaded enemy, nor as the vanquisher of Godfrey St Peter. Somehow — perhaps through the writing of the novel itself — Cather had found a type of peace, and the prospect of age and death portrayed in the *Archbishop* does not seem to trouble her. For the Archbishop himself, age comes as a mild surprise; he notices its arrival only when he looks in the mirror to shave. The slow wearing down of his body is accepted as a natural process, and he uses the enforced inactivity as an opportunity for reflection, much as Cather would later, near her own end. Illness does not upset the Archbishop. 'I shall not die of a cold, my son', he tells a young priest, 'I shall die of having lived.' There is hardly a querulous note; merely a slight displeasure at the changes he sees taking place in the world. Men travel faster these days, he tells Eusabio, but he is by no means sure that they travel to better things. None the less, he is resigned to this; it is what now lies behind that concerns him most now. 'During those last weeks of the Bishop's life he thought very little about death; it was the Past he was leaving. The future would take care of itself.' Once more, Cather sounded the note which echoed in her own heart: '. . . it was the Past he was leaving. . . '. Yet there is a change; a few years previously, it is doubtful whether she could have written that 'the future would take care of itself'.

'A novel', Cather wrote in the *Commonweal*, 'is merely a work of imagination in which a writer tries to present the experiences and emotions of a group of people by the light of his own.' Whether the *Archbishop* is a 'novel' will probably be disputed for years to come. Yet no one can deny that it is a true reflection of the light that led the author onwards at that time. Cather wrote to Ida Tarbell that writing the *Archbishop* had been the purest pleasure of her life, just as she was to write elsewhere that 'the happy mood in which I began it never paled'. When the story came to an end, she missed the Archbishop sorely. It was as if by living with Latour's graceful acknowledgement of the inevitable, made more acceptable by being set in an earlier, less destructive age, Cather herself had been enabled to come to terms with the passing of time. The triumphant tone had returned to her writing, but it was now gentler, a subdued, peaceful satisfaction of age rather than the passionate song of youth. The reader should note, however, that the voice of youth was not quite forgotten: as he lies dying, the thoughts of the Archbishop return to a field in France where, long ago, he had tried to comfort his soul's brother, Vaillant, a young man torn between the desire to go and the need to stay. Thea Kronborg, too, had suffered this torment, just as Cather herself had done. Passion, desire; these were the driving forces behind the pursuit of all great things.

It was just as well that Latour brought his creator strength and serenity when he did, for the next few years were to test Cather's new-found faith severely. While the *Archbishop* was astonishing the literary world with its simplicity and beauty, Cather learned that she was to lose her beloved Bank Street: a subway was to be driven through Greenwich Village and the old, familiar house would be torn down. For both Cather and Edith Lewis it was an upsetting time, but for Willa, the move came particularly hard. Then in her fifty-fourth year, she hated change more than ever, and the apartment had been the scene of many happy hours during the previous fifteen years. Only six years earlier she had expounded on the beauty of old houses in an interview with the *Lincoln Sunday Star*. When a friend announced that she was leaving her home of forty years, Cather was appalled: 'What better reason can you want for staying in a house than that you have lived there for forty years?. . . . The beauty lies in the associations that cluster around it, the way in which the house has fitted itself to the people.'

Still, there was no choice in the matter. Exhausted after putting their furniture into store and unable to face the search for another place, the two women took rooms at the Grosvenor Hotel on 35 Fifth Avenue, and Cather tried to console herself with the fact that the hotel was across the street from her favourite New York church. The arrangement was to have been temporary, but they were to remain there for almost five years.

The loss of Bank Street was only the first in a number of sad changes. During August of that year, 1927, Willa Cather was summoned to Red Cloud: her father had had a heart attack. After a brief but worrying interval Charles Cather seemed to recover, and his daughter returned East, cancelling her plans for a trip to Europe. She went back to Red Cloud for Christmas that year, and remained there until February. But hardly had she returned to New York than she was called home once again; her father had had another attack, and this one had been fatal. Willa Cather arrived in Red Cloud early in the morning after Charles Cather died. She entered the house and found her father in his room, lying on a couch before the bay window. There she stayed with him until the sun rose, and the other members of the family were about. It was the hardest of blows to accept, that her gentle father, so close to her in life, had now passed out of her reach forever.

Cather remained in Red Cloud for another month, while Douglass took their mother to live with him in Southern California. When she at last returned to New York, she immediately caught influenza from one of the Grosvenor's chambermaids. After spending most of the spring of 1928 recuperating, she was well enough to accept an honorary degree from Columbia University in June, then made for the solace of Grand Manan with Edith Lewis. During that sad summer, Miss Lewis wrote, Grand Manan 'seemed the only foothold left on earth. With all her things in storage — with not even a comfortable writing table to write at — Willa Cather looked forward fervently to her attic at Grand Manan'.

Due to Willa's weakened state, it was decided to bypass the usual route via Maine. Instead, they planned to take the train through Canada, via Montreal and Quebec, and from there on to St. John to catch the ferry to the island. Alas, Edith Lewis came down with flu in Quebec, and Willa Cather was left alone to explore the old Canadian city until her companion recovered. In one sense, it was a fortunate illness since it allowed Cather to make her first acquaintance with the unique atmosphere of Quebec. She wandered through the upper and lower towns, visited the Church of Notre Dame, the Ursuline Convent, the impressive Laval Seminary, bringing back glowing accounts of all she had seen to Edith Lewis. When the latter had recovered, they visited the Île d'Orléans together. It was clear that something about Quebec excited Cather, and she was to return there several times in coming years. Depressed and saddened, faced by change, death, and illness, it seems certain that Willa Cather was searching for a new project in which to lose herself; certainly, there is no record of an inner explosion for her next novel. Whatever the circumstances of her visit, it is very likely that the city of Quebec would have intrigued her in any case. For in this old city built upon its stout rock, she discovered a 'curious endurance of a kind of culture, narrow but definite'. There, another time persisted. There, she said, was an idea about life she could not wholly accept, but could none the less admire, enough to make it the subject of her new novel, *Shadows on the Rock* (1931).

Cather was fortunate to have the novel to work on. She began writing it in December 1928, the same month in which Virginia Cather suffered a stroke. The next three years proved an exhausting combination of caring for her mother and working upon the book. It is no small achievement that, by the time *Shadows on the Rock* was published in 1931, Willa Cather had crossed the continent three times to California, visited Quebec an additional three times to verify facts and, somehow, managed a trip to France — all this in the age before air travel became common. Little wonder that when, in 1930, she accepted a gold medal for *Death Comes for the Archbishop* at the American Academy of Arts and Letters, Hamlin Garland wrote that he found Willa Cather so changed as to be unrecognisable. By a sad coincidence, the book that she had begun at the time of her mother's stroke and that had sustained her throughout the long period of her illness appeared in the bookshops during the month in which Virginia Cather died.

Shadows on the Rock is not a story of death and dying, however; nor is it at all depressing. It is a novel of equilibrium, stasis, a placid portrait of a city frozen in time, as fixed and unwavering as the rock upon which it stands. The rock is that of Quebec, and the story recounts one year in the lives of the seventeenth-century colonists who make their homes upon it, their lives passing as shadows across its immutable face. It is set in a firm historical framework complete with historical figures (Count Frontenac, Bishop Laval), whose actions are accorded no more importance than those of an apothecary (Euclide Auclair) and his twelve-year-old daughter, Cécile. Most of the 'action', if such it can be called, takes place between October 1697 and November 1698. The book opens as Auclair stands beside the empty river; the last ship of the year to France has just sailed, the colony's last link with the outside world for the next eight months.

The novel is divided into six books. Book I introduces us to Auclair, a mild, almost timid, widower who has followed his patron, Count Frontenac, from France to this new country. His daughter, Cécile, is busy learning to run their household two years after her mother's death, trying to match that sense of order so important to her father — and, indeed, to the book itself. Book II follows Cécile and her six-year-old friend Jacques Gaux on their modest adventures around the town; Jacques, the son of a local prostitute, has been more or less adopted by Cécile, to whom he is sometimes a friend, sometimes a little brother. 'The Long Winter' of Book III moves on into the cold, dark months of the year, centering upon the historical and religious aspects of the society: the conflict between the new Bishop Saint-Villier, and the old Bishop Laval; the story of a Montreal recluse, Jeanne Le Ber, and her visions; the appearance of Father Hector and his tales of the Wilderness. Book IV shows us the figure of Pierre Charron, a former suiter of Jeanne Le Ber, and a loyal friend of the Auclairs. Book V describes the return of the ships from France. In Book VI, Count Frontenac dies, denied his last wish to see France again There is also an Epilogue, set twenty-five years later, which summarises the lives of the characters, contrasting the changes in the outside world with the calm domestic happiness of Cécile and Pierre, now married and with four sons. The whole book is interspersed with Quebecois legends and enough of the historical background is sketched in to provide a sense of unity.

Cather stated that, in writing *Shadows*, she had wanted to use a method similar to that achieved in the *Archbishop*, but with a difference: where the earlier book had taken the form of legend, *Shadows on the Rock* seemed more like an 'old song', incomplete but with a sympathetic, evocative and melodious setting. In a letter to William Cross, a reviewer who had the insight to understand her design, Cather wrote that she had wanted to develop the musical story into 'a prose composition not too conclusive, not too definite: a series of pictures remembered rather than experienced; a kind of thinking, a mental complexion inherited, left over from the past, lacking in robustness, and full of pious resignation'.

Where, then, in this 'fresco' of seventeenth-century Quebec, can we find the essential Willa Cather? The answer is everywhere, for, just as she described the story as a series of remembered pictures, when taken as a whole the book is like one large 'thought picture', and the thoughts are those of Willa Cather. As E.K. Brown commented: 'The novel in which Willa Cather traveled farthest from Red Cloud drew most of its emotional power from her memories of her life there during the years when that life had finally to take its place in the irreversible past'.

The loss of her apartment, her ill-health, the death of her

father, a dying mother . . . one can understand the appeal that a world which changed only slowly, that held to its strongly-rooted tradition, must have held for Cather during this period of her life. Yet *Shadows on the Rock* represents more than a search for solace or stability. Essentially, the society living in the city founded on the rock of 'Kebec' is not far removed from that of the Red Cloud of Cather's youth. Consider this passage from Book II:

> When an adventurer carries his gods with him into a remote and savage country, the colony he founds will, from the beginning, have graces, traditions, riches of the mind and spirit. Its history will shine with bright incidents, slight, perhaps, but precious, as in life itself, where the great matters are often as worthless as astronomical distances, and the trifles dear to the heart's blood.

Did not both Alexandra and Ántonia bring their own gods with them to the bleak plains of the Divide? Thea Kronborg surely takes hers with her on her journey towards her creative fulfilment. An immigrant's childhood language, a traditional recipe for brioche, a violin from Bohemia, a young musician's longing for perfect technique . . . Willa Cather always treated these 'belongings' of her characters as of equal importance, seeing them all as riches of mind and spirit. The forest surrounding the Rock is described as 'suffocation, annihilation', just as the Divide was seen as an 'erasure of personality'. Against both backgrounds the beauty of everyday events — these trifles — shines out with startling clarity and brightness. When Cécile returns home from the Harnois family, for example, where the children did not wash and where they slept in dirty sheets, she rejoices in the age-old order and traditions of her parents: 'These coppers, big and little, these brooms and clouts and brushes, were tools; and with them one made, not shoes or cabinet work, but life itself. One made a climate within a climate; one made the days, . . . one made life.'

The order and stability of the people of 'Kebec' are, perhaps, extreme, but they have their basis in that same respect for the traditions of the old order that is inherent in Cather's most fully-realised characters; thus one experiences the same feeling of hope within the offspring of Cécile and Pierre Charron as one does with Ántonia's brood: their children are the future, a perpetuation of the beauty of their own lives.

In a more personal sense, traces of Willa Cather may be found in the character of Cécile, notably in her loving relationship with her father — Auclair is just as gentle and just as blind to his daughter's growing maturity as Charles Cather had been. Cécile's love of stories and legends of the Rock is an echo of the little girl who had listened so hungrily to tales from the old women of the Divide. Cécile even shares Cather's distaste for explanations of stories. 'N'expliquez pas, chère Mère, je vous en supplie!' she says when Reverend Mother Juschereau begins to moralise. Cécile Auclair, however, is a far more pliant child than little Willie Cather would ever have been.

Cather's love of the French and French society pervades *Shadows on the Rock*. It was a love that went back many years, as is evident in her early choices of literary models as well as in her later journalism. As early as 1921, in a New York interview, she made her feelings clear:

The Frenchman doesn't talk nonsense about art, about self-expression. . . . His house, his garden, his vineyards, these are the things that fill his mind. He creates something beautiful, something lasting. And what happens? When a French painter wants to paint a picture, he makes a copy of a garden, a house, a village. The art in them inspires his brush. And twenty, thirty, forty years later, you'll find it changed only by the mellowness of time.

Willa Cather was not so insensitive to the injustices of the past, however, that her treatment of it in her novels was entirely adulatory. The decadence and inhumanities of the old French regime are not left out of *Shadows on the Rock*. There is, for example, the story of Blinker, who had been a torturer in the King's prison at Rouen before he fled to Canada, or the tragic tale of old Bichet. Her treatment of this background material is such that it is distanced from the Rock — present day events, good and evil, flow *around* the society, disturbing it very little, if at all. Auclair, for all his order, is open to new ideas, yet Catheresquely suspicious of so-called 'progress': 'Change is not always progress, Monseigneur', he tells Bishop de Saint Villier, when the latter advocates the 'modern' technique of bloodletting.

Change versus stasis, Old World versus New, stability versus mutability, love, loyalty, friendship . . . all the standard Cather themes are in the book, flowing through it like quiet rivulets. And while the small dramas and discussions are taking place, the Rock is there, eternal, a symbol of faith, security and hope; ultimately it should be seen as a religious symbol, perhaps even of God Himself. Cather's skilful handling of this difficult and delicate technique is highly successful, for the reader comes away from the novel with a sense of the surreal. One is lulled by it, hypnotised — exactly the sensation the author intended to convey. It is almost like the last thoughts of a mind on its way to a peaceful death. *Shadows on the Rock* lacks the remarkable beauty of *Death Comes for the Archbishop*. The vital force which pervaded the latter work is not present; in comparison, *Shadows* is an anti-climax, but pleasing, constructed to shine with a quiet glow rather than a flame.

The novel may not have been so artistically successful as its predecessor; nevertheless *Shadows on the Rock* outsold the *Archbishop*, a fact that surprised its author considerably. She was pleased, of course, but no amount of public acceptance could stifle the despair she now felt in her private life. In 1931 her mother died and with that death a part of her life had gone forever; the family was no longer a unit, and she had suddenly become the older generation. After spending that Christmas in Red Cloud with her brothers and sisters, she was never to return. Worse, she confessed to *feeling* like 'the older generation'; though she was only 58, the past four years had obviously taken their toll of her vitality. Others, too, noticed the lessening of creativity and lack of energy. 'During the five years at the Grosvenor', Edith Lewis wrote, 'I believe that momentum was checked — never again to regain its former drive'.

Final Weakness, Final Strength

Though the force was fading, there was still some creative spark which manifested itself in other forms. During the period of her mother's illness, Cather managed to produce four fine short stories in addition to *Shadows*, three of which were collected and published in 1932. (The fourth, 'Double Birthday', appeared in The Forum in 1929 and has never been reprinted.) *Obscure Destinies* contains the classic 'Old Mrs. Harris' (previously discussed), Cather's autobiographical account of Grandmother Boak's last days. Another tale is entitled 'Two Friends', an interesting little sketch of two Red Cloud businessmen whom Cather had known as a girl. The narrator is herself a child, between the ages of ten to thirteen; she tells the account of how two good friends grew apart and eventually split over politics.

'Neighbour Rosicky' is the happiest of the three stories. The main character is based both on Annie Pavelka's husband, and Cather's deep feelings about her own father. Brown and Woodress both suggest that the story should be seen as a sequel to *My Ántonia*, and the opinion is justified. the Bohemian family in question would seem to be that of Ántonia (here called 'Mary') some years after Jim Burden's last visit. In both the novel and the short story, 'Anton', is the name given to Cuzak and Rosicky, and the elder son in each case is 'Rudolph'. In the short story, however, the focus is on Rosicky/Cuzak rather than his wife.

When the story opens, Anton Rosicky has discovered that he has a heart condition and he is not allowed to do the labouring work on his farm. The entire Rosicky family — and Anton in particular — have prospered less than their more materialistic neighbours; but to Anton, the well-being of his family has always been more important than making money. As the doctor who examines him reflects: 'People as generous and warm-hearted and affectionate as the Rosickys never got ahead much; maybe you couldn't enjoy your life and put it in the bank, too.'

The rest of the tale follows the course of the last few months left to Rosicky: his reflections on and memories of his life, his good fortune at having escaped from the pressures of the city, and the happiness of his family. His last duty is to help to integrate his American daughter-in-law into the close-knit immigrant family circle, and this he accomplishes with his 'special gift for loving people'. When the fatal heart attack comes — as we know it must — it is his daughter-in-law, Polly, who holds his hand at the end. Written during the period between the deaths of her father and mother, the optimism that radiates from the story makes a strong contrast to the thoughtful detachment of *Shadows on the Rock*, written during the same period. Later, Cather was to admit that she had indeed been conscious of a curious split in her writing powers during the last slow weeks of her mother's illness. *Shadows* had been a quiet refuge, a place of contemplative retreat, where she could escape for a few hours concentration. But her more immediate emotions required another outlet, which she found in these stories, all drawn from various periods of her earlier life. Even 'Double Birthday', a darker, more nostalgic piece, took her back to her Pittsburg years and her contacts with singers.

Despite the darkness which had surrounded her in the last few years, there were some bright spots for Willa Cather. After her mother's death, she and Edith Lewis were finally able to look for a more agreeable place to live. From all accounts, Willa was anxious to leave New York, for by this time she detested the city. However, Edith Lewis still had a job there, so they had no option but to remain. In the end the two women settled in what was, for Cather, a rather out-of-character location: 570 Park Avenue, in the centre of one of New York's most affluent districts. Elizabeth Sergeant, a staunch supporter of the Roosevelts and their social policies, was dubious about the arrangement. Would Rosicky or Grandma Harris have been allowed past the apartment-house's uniformed attendants? Cather, however, seems to have been pleased enough with her surroundings, if a trifle embarrassed by her change of status. The unpacking of her personal treasures, the selection of a few new furnishings; the return of the beloved Josephine and her French cooking . . . these things brought great delight to the ageing author. As Edith Lewis wrote: 'It was like beginning really to live again'. Besides the comfort of being surrounded by familiar objects, the apartment's thick walls and floors gave good insulation from the street noises below and the sound of feet above; if Cather could not live away from the city, at least she could be insulated from its ugliness. And the somewhat luxurious surroundings did assure her of comfort, an important factor as she entered her sixtieth year.

Although Cather shut herself away from the city and from prying eyes, she did make a few new friends. Foremost among them were Yehudi Menuhin and his family, whom Cather had first met through the Hambourgs in France during 1930. Young Yehudi with his extraordinary talent for the violin had overturned all Willa's scepticism concerning child prodigies. Neither he nor his sisters were spoilt or self-centred. When the Menuhins stayed for a time in New York, cries of 'Aunt Willa' often filled the Park Avenue apartment. Cather took it upon herself to give the young Menuhins lessons on William Shakespeare, after she had noticed this gap in their education. For her they were like Tom Outland's 'breath of fresh air'. There were walks in Central Park, trips to the opera, birthday meals and, occasionally, some less 'refined' pleasures. In February 1934 Carrie Miner Sherwood received a letter from Willa saying (among other things) that she had been out in the park all morning sledging with Yehudi and his sisters; she was pleased to report that Yehudi stored his sled in her apartment.

The Menuhins brought music back into Willa Cather's life, an increasingly important pleasure (her one concession to the modern age was a phonograph presented to her by Alfred and Blanche Knopf). It could be that her meetings with Yehudi during 1930 and 1931 and her return to Red Cloud after Virginia Cather's death combined to produce the idea for *Lucy Gayheart*, (1935), though Edith Lewis suggests that the figure of a girl like Lucy had teased Cather's mind years before.

Cather had begun the novel after getting settled in her new apartment, that is, sometime during 1933. Yet she did not attack the story with her usual vigour; the line-a-day diary from this period contains many entries of 'very tired', or 'deadly tired', a sure sign of diminished strength. Still, Cather worked at the manuscript throughout the year, until physical misfortune intervened once more. She tore a tendon in her wrist, which meant that she was unable to write for several months — exasperating, but unavoidable — thus, the book was not completed until mid-July of 1935. It was published first as a serial in 1935, for these were the Depression years, and Cather, much as she hated serialisation, needed the extra money, both for herself and for friends in Nebraska who had fallen on hard times.

The novel that thus helped her to help others had its origins in the character of a Red Cloud girl whom Cather had once known named Sadie Becker. Sadie was lively, talented and full of energy; she had been the accompanist for a local singer. She had fallen in love, but the boy, being for some reason forbidden to see her, eventually married someone else. Sadie, for her part, left Red Cloud to study music and never returned. In Willa Cather's hands, the little incident was enlarged and given a cloak of tragedy.

Lucy, like the real-life Sadie, is an attractive girl of some talent, with a vivacious personality. People remember her as 'a slight figure always in motion', but her motion is controlled by fate. 'Some people's lives', Cather wrote, 'are affected by what happens to their person or their property; but for others fate is what happens to their feelings and their thoughts — that and nothing more.' What happens to the 'feelings and thoughts' of Lucy Gayheart, a prairie girl in Chicago to study music, is Clement Sebastian, an American-born singer. The above quotation from the story is placed after Lucy hears Sebastian sing for the first time, and experiences an unexplained feeling of foreboding.

Sebastian is an archetypal unfulfilled middle-aged artist. He is estranged from his wife, who lives in France, while he supports them both by his concert tours. Lucy, who does not care as passionately for art as did Thea Kronberg, predictably falls in love with the artist: Sebastian. He, in his turn, declares his love for her. His next European tour lies ahead, after which he plans to return to Lucy, but he dies in a boating accident before he can do so. Lucy returns to her home town of Haverford (Red Cloud), heartbroken. Shunned by her former lover, Harry Gordon, whom she rejected for Sebastian, Lucy finds little sympathy and no solace. Her depression soon lifts, however — as the reader would expect, for Lucy's character is all too shallow. At last she pulls herself together, making plans to return to Chicago and seek her fortune. After a tiff with Harry Gordon, who still refuses to acknowledge her, Lucy skates out on the river in a huff, falls through the ice and is drowned. The last pages of the novel deal with Harry's self-reproach in the years that follow.

From one point of view, the story is successful, for the character of Lucy comes off as Cather had evidently intended; she is a light-hearted, careless, rather silly young girl. Although she is made to feel the pull of compulsion, she is not able to realise it — she hasn't the drive, nor the capability for the overwhelming passion. Moreover, she has never dreamt of a 'career'; she is not inwardly creative and, indeed, is nothing more than her name suggests — a gay heart. And when that heart comes in contact with a discontented, middle-aged singer, the effect is similar to that of Hilda Burgoyne upon Bartley Alexander. Predictably, like Bartley, and Willa Cather herself, Clement Sebastian despairs of his lost youth: 'Nothing had ever made Sebastian admit to himself that his youth was forever and irrevocably gone. He had clung to a secret belief that he could pick it up again, somewhere'. Most of his musings reflect Cather's own state of mind: 'Life had so turned out that now, when he was nearing fifty, he was without a country, without a home, without a family, and very nearly without friends.'

The passing of the years had seen Willa Cather through many similar situations, though none, perhaps, quite so extreme. Yet it is clear that Sebastian is a displaced figure, just as Cather felt herself to be. The themes within the novel are familiar Cather country and could have resulted in some masterful work but that the gentle glow which pervaded *Shadows on the Rock* had been finally extinguished. Cather could find no real enthusiasm for it, and the result is flat in comparison to her other works. The plot is a repetition, a reversal of Thea Kronborg's story. Also, Cather had neither known nor loved her prototype enough; Sadie Becker was only an acquaintance. The book is effective, particularly in the scenes in Haverford, but no more than that. One of the chief faults is the predictability of the plot; its foreshadowing — use of images of drowning, Byron's 'When we two parted', and so on — is too blatant. Almost from the beginning the alert reader knows how the story will end. There is also an atypical tendency towards sentimentality throughout the novel. It is interesting to note, however, that the Catherian traditions remain the same: both Lucy and Sebastian are American and both die, defeated, to join the ranks of the other 'lost' characters. But these two are even greater losers, because they lack the fire of their predecessors. Even this quality reflects the author's mental state, for Lucy Gayheart was the one character Willa Cather ever admitted losing patience with; she grew tired of Lucy, just as she was to grow tired of more and more things during this period.

Things were not going well for Cather. During the Bank Street years, when her physical surroundings had been no more than adequate, her work and her life had flowed harmoniously, with continuity and force. The force turned to bitterness at times, but it was a creative one none the less. Now, surrounded by the material comforts of Park Avenue, life again became difficult for her. With her energy at an ebb, she suffered from frequent physical complaints that made proper writing impossible. The worst was yet to come.

In March 1935, Isabelle McClung Hambourg returned to America, in hopes of finding a medical miracle for what became a terminal illness. While Jan travelled the country giving concerts, Willa spent most of her time visiting Isabelle in the hospital. When Isabelle had recovered enough to join her husband in Chicago, Willa accompanied her there, then followed the Hambourgs to Europe in August. When she parted from Isabelle to return to New York, Willa Cather knew that she would probably never see her dearest friend again.

In 1936 Cather was sixty-three years of age. That year she brought out only *Not Under Forty*, a book of essays all of which (barring one on Thomas Mann) had been published previously; some had been expanded for inclusion in the collection. Sarah Orne Jewett, Mrs Fields and Katherine Mansfield are discussed; the famous 'Novel Démeublé' is included; there is also a pleasing account of a meeting Cather had had with Mme Franklin Grout, the niece of her admired Flaubert, in 1930. Throughout the volume, one can sense Cather's mood of the 1930s, her penultimate decade. The book is for 'the backward', she wrote in the Preface (meaning those over forty), having been written by one of their number. There is a tone of mixed nostalgia, gentle pontification, and defensiveness. In 'A Chance Meeting', Cather takes a jab at all those exasperating reporters who had ever pestered her own privacy. Mme Grout evidently talked extensively to Cather; there were hints of letters from Turgenev. 'But these were very personal memories', she wrote, 'and if Madame Grout had wished to make them public, she would have written them herself.' The pages are filled with statements concerning youth and age, art and simplicity and values, and may be seen as providing a summing-up of one writer's beliefs by the writer herself.

She wrote one other short story that year ('The Old Beauty'). Most of 1937 was taken up by the preparation of a complete edition of her works — a task that both upset and irritated her, for it took all of her time. The project did give her the opportunity to cut, delete, and rearrange her works as much as she liked, however, for which she was grateful. It was this same instinct for control that made her reluctant to have her letters published or her works dramatised or anthologised after her death: she would not be around to supervise the selection or adaptation, a right, she felt, that belonged to every artist.

During that autumn Cather managed to begin, after a long delay, the only one of her novels to use the Southern material of her earliest childhood. This is *Sapphira and the Slave Girl*, on which she worked throughout the winter of 1937/8. A trip to Virginia was then proposed and so, that spring, Willa Cather and Edith Lewis set off for Winchester. Lewis has recorded her impressions of that journey, watching the effect this homecoming had upon her companion:

> It was a memorable experience, as intense and thrilling in its way, as those journeys to New Mexico, when she was writing the *Archbishop*. Every bud and leaf and flower seemed to speak to her with a peculiar poignancy. . . . She found again the wild azalea growing on the gravelly banks of the road up Timber Ridge, and gathered great bunches of it. . . . Her delight in these things gave, I think, a great freshness of detail to *Sapphira*.

There were many changes; Willow Shade itself was run down, the willows had been done away with and the familiar box hedge was gone. But Cather, Lewis wrote, refused to see the change: 'She looked through and through it, as if it were transparent, to what she knew as its reality.' Instead of disheartening her the transformation lit another inner flame, a very prolific one, for the flood of memories released was so great that Cather's first draft was twice as long as the finished novel.

Although Cather began writing *Sapphira and the Slave Girl* during 1937, the book was not published until 1940; the delay was not of her choice. During that time she had to face the loss of several people dear to her; indeed it is extraordinary that *Sapphira* was written at all.

In June 1938, out of the blue, Douglass Cather died of a heart attack; Willa had seen him six months before, when the brother and sister had spent Christmas together. As the eldest, Willa had assumed her siblings would outlive her; the shock of Douglass's death was such that she couldn't bring herself to attend his funeral. Before she had even begun to come to terms with this loss, word reached her that Isabelle Hambourg had also died — just four months after Douglass.

Numb, shocked with grief, Willa Cather went that autumn to

Jaffrey for solace, only to find that a hurricane had destroyed much of its beautiful woodlands. The following year saw the outbreak of the Second World War. On the day in June 1940 when France fell to the Germans, Cather's diary contained this entry: 'There seems to be no future at all for people of my generation.'

During this traumatic period Cather clung to *Sapphira* desperately, throwing herself into it, often working far beyond her strength. Despite death, disaster and war, the novel was completed in time for Knopf's Christmas trade in December 1940. It was published on Cather's 67th birthday.

'Austere', 'cool', 'lacking in passion . . .' — these are some of the adjectives that have been applied to the story. Yet though it seems to lack outward passion, the reader can still sense the powerful emotional undercurrents running through the novel, just below the surface, and the reserved tone which Cather employs perfectly supports the main character, Sapphira Dodderidge Colbert. Indeed, most of the cuts to the original manuscript were made so that Sapphira herself might occupy the central place.

Sapphira's story, set in pre-Civil War Virginia, may, like the *Archbishop* or *Shadows*, seem atypical for such a personal writer as Willa Cather. But, as in the other novels, Cather responded to both the main character and the story as a whole for two reasons: first, the saga has all been lived before; and, second, it came directly from the Cather family archives, being based on Cather's own great-grandparents, her Grandmother Boak (Rachel Blake) and of course upon Nancy and Till, who appear in the novel without so much as a name change.

Most of the novel's action occurs during the year 1856. Sapphira Colbert is seen to be a Southern matriarch in her twilight years; a proud, powerful, rather imperious figure, she commands respect. Although confined to the house, being wheelchair-bound, she still manages both house and farm, ruling the roost just as she has always done. Her husband is Henry Colbert, a hardworking but rather passive man, who evidently likes things that way. 'You're the master here and I'm the miller', he tells his wife, and the statement sums up their relationship: each partner has a separate realm, living, for the most part, independently of one another: Henry even sleeps down at his mill.

The Colbert marriage had been sealed under strange circumstances; when Sapphira married Henry she took a step down on the social ladder. To escape from speculation and gossip, she, her passive husband and twenty slaves moved from her previous high social standing in Loudon County to an inherited property in the poorer region of Back Creek. Although the change of location was over a relatively short distance, the move, combined with Henry's Flemish ancestry, has the effect of giving the Colberts an immigrant role in Back Creek, coming in as they do from a much richer society: they are indeed a 'strange couple to be found on Back Creek'. The fact that Sapphira owns slaves — though her husband does not agree with the practice — only serves to make the alienation complete, for the Back Creek community is in non-slave-holding territory.

Rachel Blake, the only child of the Colberts, is a widow who lives not far from Mill House (Willow Shade) with her two small daughters. The subject of slavery is even more detestable to her than it is to her father, and it is and has been a constant source of conflict between mother and daughter, eventually coming to a head when Rachel helps a slave to escape. For Sapphira, however, who has been brought up with it, slavery is a natural circumstance; she cannot understand what so upsets her daughter, and puts it all down to plain stubbornness: 'Rachel had always been difficult, — rebellious toward the fixed ways which satisfied other folk. Mrs. Colbert had been heartily glad to get her married and out of the house at seventeen. . . '. In contrast to her mother's life of comparative luxury, Rachel lives a life of constant service as a nurse to the poor mountain folk of the community. Needless to say, her chosen poverty is another constant source of irritation to Sapphira.

As the book opens, the question of slavery is the cause of a dispute between husband and wife. Among the many slaves at Mill House is a pretty young mulatto named Nancy, the daughter of old Till, Sapphira's ladies' maid. As with so many active people suddenly forced into an inactive existence through disability, Sapphira's mind works overtime, feeding upon its own suspicions. When one morning, at breakfast, she suddenly announces her intention to sell Nancy, Henry Colbert for once stands up to her and refuses to permit it: Nancy looks after him down at the mill, and the two share an innocent, almost father/

daughter relationship. Henry's refusal preys upon Sapphira's mind, and the portrayal of her character provides a fascinating case study.

Although not naturally vicious (we do not witness the sharp, almost constant malevolence of a Myra Henshawe) Sapphira is none the less calculating. Determined to punish both her husband and Nancy for a gentle happiness in which she has no part, Sapphira treats the situation as if it were all a kind of cold, spiteful game. Like an old spider, she patiently bides her time, spinning out a web in which to ensnare Nancy, until the poor young woman becomes a pawn in what emerges as a dangerous chess match. Sapphira invites Martin Colbert, Henry's nephew and a notorious rake, to Mill House. By assigning Nancy to serve him, she creates ample opportunity for Martin to rape the girl: at first Nancy is made to sleep outside Sapphira's door in the hall, where she is clearly vulnerable; later Nancy is sent into the woods to gather laurel — just before Martin sets off in the same direction. In desperation, the girl appeals to Rachel Blake, who eventually smuggles her out of the South on the underground railroad.

All this time, Henry Colbert has been far too passive to confront the issue; when he finally does so, he cannot save Nancy himself. Like most of Cather's male characters, he lacks the strength to face up to a difficult or uncomfortable situation. When his daughter eventually convinces him that Martin will ruin Nancy, Henry, at first, protests:

'No he won't! It's only by the mercy of God I haven't strangled the life out of him before now.'
'Then why don't you do something to save her?'
He made no reply.

Henry does, admittedly, provide money for Nancy's escape, but even then he does so in a cowardly fashion, leaving some bills in his coat pocket and telling Rachel that the coat will be hanging by his window.

Nancy goes successfully, fearfully, to safety. Rachel is at first estranged from her mother, but after the death of one of her granddaughters Sapphira relents, inviting Rachel and her remaining grandchild to move up to the 'big house'. An Epilogue set twenty-five years later recounts the moving moment when

Nancy is at last able to return to her old mother, Till.

Besides beautiful description and a sensitive handling of characterisation, Cather showed remarkable insight and justice in her treatment of the slavery issue. Had the author of *Sapphira* been a woman such as Elizabeth Sergeant, steeped in Eastern reform movements, the story could easily have turned into a polemic. Cather, however, was a Southerner by birth, a Mid-Westerner by experience and almost a European by taste; the same qualities of sympathy and objectivity that enabled her to praise and damn a Nebraskan town within the same paragraph allowed her to deal justly with a delicate subject.

Cather provides Sapphira, to whom slavery is an accepted part of life, with a disapproving husband as a counterbalance. Henry Colbert is opposed to slavery, in many ways, he is also wise enough to realise that the system cannot be completely and suddenly ended. Indeed, when he offers freedom to Sampson, his black head miller, the latter declines in horror: he has heard stories about the 'free' North, and the slow death of the poor there in ghettoes and factories; why should he want to exchange one kind of poverty for another? The Mill House is his home, and with a 'good' master such as Henry Colbert, Sampson is reasonably happy. Henry realises that, in one sense, Sampson is right: the Colbert slaves are better fed and cared for than the poor mountain whites. Yet what mountain man would want to trade places with Sampson?

For her part, Sapphira is normally a good mistress to work for — she does not beat her slaves, although in a fit of frustrated temper she does strike Nancy once, supposedly for not setting her hair properly. When Jezebel, Till's mother, lies dying in her shack, Sapphira makes sure that she is well looked after and visits the ancient African herself. Her relationship with Till is one of genuine affection. Every Christmas, the men on the place come up to the house for a hot toddy, which Sapphira herself serves them, and when a half-witted field-hand repeatedly runs off, she takes no retaliatory action: Sapphira wants her Negroes to be as happy and contented as possible. She knows how to manage them, however, and has repeated run-ins with Fat Lizzie, the cook.

Cather uses Lizzie to make an important point. As Henry puzzles over the problem of slavery, and the lack of Biblical guidance on the subject, he muses: 'If Lizzie, the cook, was in bonds to Sapphira, was she not almost equally in bonds to Lizzie?' Willa Cather realised that the system of slavery was a double bondage; that Sapphira, for all her dominant position, was none the less as dependent upon her slaves for the necessities of life — indeed, to stay alive — as they were on her for their protection and sustenance. Cather did not have to like the system — indeed, the attitudes expressed in the novel make it clear that she did not — yet she could understand the reasons behind its existence. 'No, it ain't put on', Cather has Rachel Blake say of her mother's faith in the system. 'She believes in it, and they believe in it. But it ain't right.' Yet only the younger slaves, such as Nancy, are the ones fully able to accept and benefit from freedom. For the older slaves like Till, who in some way believe in the old order themselves, freedom would be an unspeakable tragedy. They could not learn to adapt, just as old Peter Sadilek or Papa Shimerda could not. Willa Cather realised this fact, as she shows in the reconciliatory conversation between Henry and Sapphira, after Sapphira has at last invited Rachel back home.

> 'You are a kind woman', [Henry tells her.] 'You are good to a great many folks, Sapphy.'
> 'Not so good as Rachel with her basket!' [Sapphira replies.]
> 'There are different ways of being good to folks', the miller held out stubbornly. . . . 'Sometimes keeping people in their place is being good to them.'

In addition to being a study in character, *Sapphira and the Slave Girl* is also a study in tradition. Like *Shadows on the Rock*, it portrays the survival of an old order, one with which Willa Cather did not agree but one that she could none the less understand; perhaps *Sapphira* appears more successful than *Shadows* because the material from which it was created was drawn from its author's inherited past. She was closer to it, it had come to her through family tradition, just as the old stories of the Divide had come to life when told by the pioneers themselves. Although some may consider it a 'cool' book, the reception that followed the appearance of *Sapphira* was warm indeed. Cather's tone of triumphant confidence had returned with an increased if different strength, and several critics welcomed the renewal, and praised the book highly.

For Willa Cather, however, the effort of that success brought more inflamed tendons in her hand, and soon she was admitted to a hospital in New York, returning with a brace she was to wear for the next eight months. Although the injury prohibited her from writing, Cather did not stop work altogether. There were always a great number of letters to be acknowledged, by dictation if need be: letters from anonymous fans as well as those from more prominent admirers, such as Justice Holmes. And, of course, there was always the correspondence with close friends such as Carrie Miner Sherwood or Zoë Akins; letters such as these became increasingly dear to her.

In spite of the inconvenience caused by the brace (she could not even dress herself unaided), Willa Cather wanted to make one last journey West to visit her brother Roscoe; he had been ill during the spring of 1941 and she was fearful of losing him. So she and Edith Lewis headed for San Francisco in June, crossing the familiar territories of New Mexico and Arizona. Recent rains had transformed the landscape into a fresh, green paradise, even more beautiful than they remembered. Willa Cather wept to see it. 'She knew', Edith Lewis wrote, 'that she was seeing it for the last time.'

The visit to Roscoe, apparently a very happy time, was to be the last of its kind as well, for Roscoe Cather died in 1945. The joyful reunion of that summer, however, sparked off a delicate little story of remembrance, entitled 'The Best Years', which Cather completed shortly before Roscoe's death. Edith Lewis says that Willa wrote the story purposely for her brother, to remind him of the golden days of their shared childhood. The tale is indeed a beautiful rendering of a sister/brother relationship, derived from the years when Willa, Roscoe and Douglass had shared their private lives under the eaves in their attic bedroom.

'The Best Years' tells the story of Lesley Fergusson, a young girl of sixteen who returns to her home for a weekend after accepting her first teaching post. She is totally wrapped up in her four brothers, whom she misses terribly while she is away; the top storey of the Fergusson household reveals that same attic bedroom that Cather and her brothers had shared, complete with a partition for her own room. After her visit, which is described almost entirely in terms of the sibling relationships, Lesley returns to her school; she dies there during a winter snowstorm.

When her former superintendent visits the Fergusson family twenty years later, she is pleased to find that the boys have all grown into fine men who continue to cherish the memory of their sister. Cather has Lesley's mother make a statement that summed up her own ideas about life's happiness: ' . . . our best years are when we're working hardest and going right ahead when we can hardly see our way out' — just like Cather's own years of striving in Pittsburgh and the years of creative zeal at Bank Street. The statement is an echo of an earlier line from *My Ántonia*, when Jim Burden is translating lines from the *Georgics* at college: 'Optima dies . . . prima fugit: the best days are the first to flee.'

Although she was convinced of the truth of these maxims, Cather's own last years were neither very hard nor very sad; they were, in general, years of reflection and living day by day, punctuated now and again by larger events. In 1941 there had been the visit to Roscoe; the Japanese bombing of Pearl Harbor took America into the war. In 1942, there were enjoyable visits from the Menuhins during the early part of the year; the latter part was taken up by illness. Cather underwent a gall-bladder operation and, although she did not become a complete invalid, she never fully recovered her strength. Because of the war, the yearly retreat to Grand Manan was no longer possible, so Cather and Edith Lewis adopted North Harbor, Maine, as a haven. It was there, at the Asticou Inn, that Cather finally discovered Sir Walter Scott's Waverley novels; both Virginia Cather and Judge McClung had tried to persuade her to read them, but at the time Cather had thought them dry and boring. Now, however, she was enchanted with them, and they provided her with many hours of contented reading.

During the next few years, Cather worked off and on at a novel set in mediaeval Avignon, but she did not make much headway; her hand and arm were still troublesome and she was constantly using the brace. She managed to make one last public appearance in 1944 to receive a gold medal from the National Institute of Arts and Letters; she shared the stage with S.S. McClure and flung her arms around him with something of her old verve. With the death of her brother Roscoe in 1945, however, something finally broke within her. She could not bear any more deaths; she was unable to write any more. Thus 'The Best Years' and 'Before

Breakfast', another story written in 1944, were the last works she completed. Yet in spite of the weariness and sadness, her last months seem to have been reasonably contented ones, filled with small pleasures: visits, when possible, to old friends; the never-ending stream of letters; gifts of flowers; recordings by her friend Yehudi Menuhin; a surprise visit from one of her nieces. . . . She also read a great deal, returning, so Edith Lewis tells us, almost exclusively to Chaucer and to Shakespeare, as if through the humanity and profundity of these great writers she could some-how prepare for the future. Like her own Archbishop Latour, Willa Cather used her final months as a period in which to reflect on her life and its achievements; a letter to Zoë Akins dating from 1945 reveals that, for the most part, she was satisfied with the path her career had taken. It had been a long and at times uphill struggle, this continuous birth.

Death took her gently, almost unawares. Early in April 1947 there were tentative plans for another summer trip and the possibility of some more writing. On 24 April she stayed in bed all morning, a little tired but otherwise quite normal in mood and appearance. Medical reports showed that she died late that afternoon, probably from a cerebral haemorrhage; her body was buried four days later, in Jaffrey's Old Cemetery, on a quiet hillside.

It seems fitting to let Edith Lewis, her close companion for so many years, speak her epitaph:

She was never more herself than on the last morning of her life — . . . . Her spirit was as high, her grasp of reality as firm as always. And she had kept that warmth of heart, that youthful, fiery generosity which life so often burns out.

She was a little tired that morning; full of winning courtesy to those around her; fearless, serene — with the childlike simplicity which had always accompanied her greatness; giving and receiving happiness.

Truly, like her Archbishop before her, Willa Cather died of having lived.

Notes

Where quotations from Willa Cather's own works are concerned, I have not given fuller references if the source of the quotation is quite clear; the same applies to references in the principal biographies. For purposes of identification, I have used the following abbreviations throughout:

WC	Willa Cather
EL	Edith Lewis, *Willa Cather Living*
ESS	Elizabeth Shepley Sergeant, *Willa Cather: A Memoir*
WWC	Mildred Bennett, *The World of Willa Cather*
KA	*The Kingdom of Art*
WP	*The World and the Parish*
WCHC	*Willa Cather and her Critics*
SOJ	Sarah Orne Jewett
GS	George Seibel, 'Miss Willa Cather from Nebraska' (also as MWCFN)
NUF	*Not Under Forty*
OW	*On Writing*
CSF	*Collected Short Fiction*

References to Brown, Woodress, Rascoe etc. are to the titles listed in the Bibliography below.

1: *First Impressions*

The opening quote, now so well-known, comes from an interview in *The Bookman*, as cited in *WP*, p. 50, note 22. WC was to state this in several different ways throughout her lifetime: see Hockett interview in *KA*, also ESS, p. 11. 'Nebraska' phrase is the title of GS's *Colophon* article. 'Older world' — from *Philadelphia Record* interview (9 August 1913, signed 'FH'), repr. in *KA*, p. 449. Information on Cather family origins evidently came to WC via English cousins; this seems plausible given the instance of twins in the family. WC made use of twins in some novels and stories: *A Lost Lady*; 'Old Mrs Harris'. Material on Virginia years comes from Bennett, Lewis and Woodress. Fairfax reference, see *Sapphira*, p. 23. All 'Old Mrs Harris' quotations come from *Obscure Destinies*. 'Cato' story comes from EL, p. 10, as does the description of Charles Cather, p. 5. *Journal* vignette appears in *WP*, p. 20. WC and mother's temperament, see EL, p. 7; Woodress, p. 23. For basis of Wheeler parents, see ESS, pp. 14–15. WC's naming has been the subject of a good deal of debate over the years; EL, WWC, and Woodress offer varying viewpoints. Margie/

Mahailey description comes from *One of Ours*. 'Haunting the mind' appears in 'FH' interview (above) in *KA*

2: *The Beginnings of Awareness*

For reasons behind the Cather migration, see Brown, p. 16, and Woodress p. 26. TB problems are recounted in Bennett and Woodress. 'Macon Prairie' is to be found in *April Twilights and Other Poems* (1923). 'New world' quotation and description of Nebraska — derived from WC's own account in 'Nebraska: The End of the First Cycle'. This essay also reveals some of WC's early feelings about her Southern heritage, as well as her dismay at modern materialism. The interview selections come from the 'FH' interview in *KA* (pp. 448–9). Slote discusses WC's blending of reality and imagination in 'The Secret Web' (*Five Essays on Willa Cather*); there was also the incident with the Stephen Crane article ('When I Knew Stephen Crane', reprinted in *WP*; Slote discusses the article in *KA*, 'Writer in Nebraska'); the fictional 'James' of the Burne-Jones travel article (see *WC in Europe*); both ESS and EL indicate that WC saw only what she wished. 'Happiness and curse' from interview by Eva Mahoney (*Omaha World Herald*, 27 Nov. 1921) repr. in *WWC*, p. 140. 'Flowers' from Eleanor Hinman interview (*Lincoln Sunday Star*, 6 Nov. 1921) repr. in *WWC*, p. 142. 'Daubs of color' from 'Nebraska' essay, as is attitude to foreigners; acknowledgement statement found in 'FH' (*KA*) as is the following quotation. Detailed information on WC's reading material may be found in *KA*, pp. 38–41; see also EL and *WP*. The Pittsburgh column was one of WC's 'Old Books and New' pieces (June 1897) written for the *Home Monthly*, cited in *WP*, p. 352. 'Wagner Matinee' quotes come from *CSF*. 'Flash' is cited in *WWC*, p. 75, as is *Journal* quote, p. 94. 'Curiosity Shop' comes from Brown. WC's school life is recorded in *WWC*. 'Library' quote comes from 'Old Mrs. Harris' in *Obscure Destinies*, as does the next passage. For details of the private library, see *KA*.

Concerning Howard Pyle: when the *Troll Garden* was published in 1905, WC sent Pyle a copy inscribed: 'Will Mr Howard Pyle accept through me the love of seven big and little children to whom he taught the beauty of language and of line, and to whom, in a desert place, he sent the precious message of Romance' (in the *Colophon*, Vol. 1, 1939). 'All over the country' comes from Hinman interview (above) in *WWC*. Childhood games, life etc. taken from *WWC*. All quotes regarding Mrs Miner come from *My Ántonia*. Both interviews in *WWC*, p. 77, 109. For Carrie Miner Sherwood, see Gerber, p. 24. High school speech, see Brown, pp. 44–6, also Slote's 'Secret Web' (*Five Essays*).

3: *Awakening*

Information on the University of Nebraska and Lincoln is drawn largely from Slote's 'Writer in Nebraska', *KA*, pp. 3ff. The *Semi-Centennial Anniversary Book of the University of Nebraska 1869-1919* also contains material concerning the founding of the college and its structure with photos of the early campus. Atmosphere quote comes from *KA*, p. 7. WC's wish for Rome is cited in *WWC*, pp. 112–13. See *KA*, EL and Woodress for material regarding WC's course work. 'Scrubwoman' story comes from EL, p. 30. Other accounts of WC's college days come from Woodress, Brown, and Shively (*Writings from WC's Campus Years*); the latter contains the Grace Morgan Reily letter and others which are not so flattering. A letter from Dorothy Canfield Fisher appears in *WWC*, stating emphatically that WC had many friends who loved and admired her. Westermann story comes from Brown; quotes are from Shively letters (descriptions). Dislike of flowery writing: essay to W.O. Jones, published in *Journal*, 24 July 1927, cited Woodress, p. 55. The Carlyle essay is reprinted in *KA*, pp. 424–5; this is the *Hesperian* version. The next passage from the Shakespeare essay is also repr. in *KA*, p. 434. 'Fear' found in *Early Stories of WC*. Gere story comes from *WWC*, p. 216. Westermann validates the Erlich depiction in his letter to Shively, p. 134. Moore relationship is recounted in *WP*, p. 98. 'Bow-wow' comes from Brown, p. 55. 'Peter' quote appears in *CSF*. Letters to Mariel Gere are housed at the Nebraska State Historical Society; this one is paraphrased in Woodress, p. 76.

All the early stories may be found in *Early Stories of Willa Cather*. Letter to Mrs Goudy is paraphrased in EL, p. 32. *Record* quote cited in *KA*, pp. 14–15. The quotations from WC's columns are reprinted in *WP* and *KA* and may be located via the indexes.

Details of the 'mystery meeting' with Axtell are given in *WP*, note p. 305; *KA*, p. 29; and Brown, p. 73. Byrne lists Axtell's Christian name as 'James'. All others refer to 'Charles'.

4: *Interlude*

Letters to Mariel Gere, cited in Woodress (p. 75) and *WP* (p. 306) indicate WC's homecoming sensations. 'Dreadful dirt' epithet is from letter to Gere as well, cited in *WP*, p. 375. See WC's Pittsburg columns in *WP* for her initial reactions to the city. *Home Monthly* as 'trashy' comes from Byrne, p. 8. For WC's views on women's magazines, see *KA*, pp. 187–9. On practice of using pen names, see note in *WP*, p. 306; WC's own use of pen names is discussed in *WP*, GS, and in John Hinz's 'WC in Pittsburgh' (*New Colophon*, III, 1950); some errors in assigning pseudonyms to Cather have been made, however; see also *Sixteen Modern American Authors*. 'Tommy' appears in *CSF*. On women's clubs, see letter to Mariel Gere (4 Aug. 1906), cited in *WP*, p. 504. Byrne suggests possible enmity within *Home Monthly* staff as reason for WC's resignation. For nickname and boyfriends, see Byrne. Proposals of marriage referred to in letters to Mariel Gere, cited in Woodress, p. 85; also 'male loves' theory, p. 86. *The Mill on the Floss* review appears in *WP*, p. 363 (Old Books and

New column). Seibel's description and impressions of WC are recorded in 'Miss Willa Cather from Nebraska'. On the Slack home, see EL, p. 47. 'Youth and art' column in *WP* p. 672. 'Gods' in *KA*, p. 160. Nethersole and Fiske remarks date from 1897 and are to be found in *WP*. Seibel reference from MWCFN, as is the 'eyes in every pore' statement. Illness anecdote is found in EL.

The relationship between WC and Isabelle McClung has been a subject of much speculation. Woodress calls Isabelle the 'one great romance' of WC's life (pp. 86–7), and states that the nature of the friendship had main outlines which were 'clear enough'. Although Byrne suggests the trouble caused by WC's move into the McClung household, she also makes the point that 'no evidence whatsoever has yet been adduced that the relationship was anything other than that of close friendship' (see *Chrysalis*, Chap. 4). Sharon O'Brien (*Willa Cather: The Emerging Voice*) deals explicitly with the subject of lesbianism, based in part on some letters to Louise Pound which have recently come to light.

Again, column references may be found in *WP* through the index. 'Eric' was not the first story *Cosmopolitan* had wanted; the magazine had tried to buy 'Tommy' but it had already been reserved for *Home Monthly*. Quotes from 'Eric' are found as it is listed in *Early Stories*. The critic, according to Bennett, was Eugene von Tempsky, who translated 'Eric' into German (see *Early Stories*, p. 215). The other five stories published in 1900 were: 'The Dance at Chevalier's'; 'The Sentimentality of William Taverner'; 'The Affair at Grover Station', 'A Singer's Romance'; and 'The Conversion of Sum Loo'. All appeared in the ill-fated *Library*: 'Chevalier's' under the favoured pseudonym 'Henry Nicklemann' which, GS says, came from Hauptmann's *Die Versunkene Glocke* (*The Sunken Bell*); see MWCFN. Theatre season review, the *Index* (16 Feb. 1901), as printed in *WP*, p. 794.

On the sharing of rooms with Isabelle, there are varying accounts; see Byrne, ESS, and others. For description of WC's Nebraska/East Coast conflict, see ESS, p. 49. GS had become editor of the *Gazette* in 1901. WC's travel articles appear in *WC in Europe*; also, more accurately in *WP*. Other accounts of the trip come from EL, ESS, and Brown. For a good study of WC's poetry, see Slote's 'WC and Her First Book' in the revised edition of *April Twilights* (1968). 'Grave question' is found in *KA*, p. 348. The Slote quote comes from *April Twilights* commentary, p. ix. 'Merit without greatness' in *KA*, p. 348. 'In Media Vita' and 'Prairie Dawn' excerpts both come from the original *April Twilights* (1903). The later lines from 'Going Home (Burlington Route)' were printed in *April Twilights and Other Poems* (1923). 'Stray copies' quote in ESS, pp. 182–3. For account of McClure's discovery, see Woodress. Part of the 'Roman and the Teuton' is repr. in *KA*, which also contains a discussion of it, p. 93. Cather's comments on the Rossetti poem may be found in her article repr. in *WP*, p. 143. 'Sculptor's Funeral' quotes are taken from the version printed in *CSF*. Reinhart article is in *WP*; ESS quote is on p. 61. For Seibel's preference and discussion, see MWCFN.

5: *Turning-Point*

The Louise Bogan article, 'American Classic', originally published in the *New Yorker* (8 Aug. 1931), is repr. in *WCHC*, p. 130. Moorhead's 'The Novelist', originally published in *These Too Were Here: Louise Homer and Willa Cather* (Pittsburg, University of Pittsburg Press, 1950), also repr. in part in *WCHC*, p. 106. It is assumed that the 'muckraker' term comes from an allusion in Bunyan's *Pilgrim's Progress*: 'A man could look no way but downwards with a muckrake in his hand'. The movement towards exposing scandal and social reform lasted until around 1912.

Ida Tarbell (1857–1944) worked at *McClure's* from 1894 to 1906. Lincoln Steffens (1866–1936) served as managing editor of the magazine from 1901 to 1906. Both left *McClure's* in 1906 during the first great walkout, the result of a quarrel over S.S. McClure's mismanagement of funds; S.S. promptly hired new staff, including WC, to take their place. WC's disregard of reformers and social movements is well documented in letters and friends' reminiscences; see especially **ESS**, pp. 35–7, 42–3, 166, 261. WC's own account of her meeting with Annie Fields may be found in the section '148 Charles Street', in *NUF*. All quotations come from this essay. Material on SOJ is also in *NUF*, in section 'Miss Jewett'; the long passage comes from p. 83, the next quotation from p. 80. All letter quotations come from *The Letters of SOJ* (1911). The 8 - pager is mentioned in Woodress (p. 133); it is housed at Harvard. WC's admission of financial stability is in contradiction of EL's statement, p. 67. Psychiatric help recounted in ESS. The story of WC meeting ESS is told by ESS, and the quotation is from the same source.

'Executive' quote comes from Wilson, *McClure's Magazine and the Muckrakers*, p. 187, as does the 'yes man' comment, note p. 235. On 'literary' see Moorhead's article in *WCHC*. Article in the *Colophon* by WC, 'My First Novels (There Were Two)', is repr. in *OW*. See Woodress on WC's age and experience; he states that *Alexander's Bridge* marks 'the end of her beginning'. H.L. Mencken, however, called *AB* 'full of promise'; Maxwell Geismar said it was 'a remarkably interesting first novel'; and EL rightfully defends the book in her memoir. The account of the 'Bohemian Girl' is in ESS. 'Reporter' statement comes from 'Miss Jewett' in *NUF*, p. 81.

6: *Arrival*

Hinman interview in *WWC*, pp. 76–7. See ESS for a full account of WC's return to Nebraska and the encounter with the West, pp. 79–84. The Winslow episode is reported in Brown, Lewis and Sergeant. 'Imagination' defined in an interview by Ethel Hockett (*Lincoln Daily Star*, 24 Oct. 1915), repr. in *KA*. Woodress discusses WC's mistaken imagination on pp. 177–8. 'Flesh and blood', from interview with Eva Mahoney (*Nebraska Sunday World-Herald*, Oct. 1921) cited in *WWC*, p. xi. For genesis of the 'Mulberry Tree', see ESS. 'Prairie Spring' appears as it is published in *O Pioneers!*

Cycle of Triumph — Déclassé quote taken from *OW*, p. 94. 'Skeleton' argument is told by ESS, p. 97. The move is recounted in EL, pp. 86–9. Anna Olivia (Olive) Fremstad (1871–1951) was born in Stockholm and moved to the US at the age of 10; after training in Germany and touring European cities, she made her New York debut as Sieglinde in Wagner's *Die Walküre*. In her eleven years at the Metropolitan Opera House, she sang chiefly Wagnerian roles. The statement about the *Lark* is taken from the Preface to the 1932 edition. The Heinemann statement is recorded in *OW*, p. 96. See account of the Mesa Verde trip in EL: EL quote, p. 101; quote from ESS, p. 49. For the effect of Isabelle's engagement, see ESS, p. 140. Woodress points to other reactions. Rascoe's impressions of WC are recorded in his *Bookman's Daybook*, pp. 206–8; visit to ESS recorded ibid. On Annie as artist, see Hinman interview in *WWC*, p. 46. The 'Novel Démeublé' quote appears in *OW*, p. 40.

Bridging the Present — 'Prairie Boy' in *Omaha World* interview cited in ESS, p. 172, as is the following 'as well as she knew herself' statement. For Hochstein, see *New York Herald* interview (24 Dec. 1922), repr. in ESS, pp. 174ff. On *One* taking a lot out of WC, see *WWC*. Woodress points to letters in which WC expresses her uncertainty about the book. Quote on 'right to do so' is from an *Omaha World* interview, cited in ESS.

Cycle of Defeat — 'World broke in two' occurs in the prefaratory note. See especially ESS for WC's reaction to the new era. 'Novel Démeublé quote in *NUF*, p. 50. Somerset Maugham's opinion is reported by Rascoe, p. 132. For ESS's sketch, see ESS, p. 11; EL passage comes from p. 135. For records of WC's illnesses, see Brown, EL and Woodress. Grattan's statement comes from his Preface to a *Bookman's Daybook*, p. xiv. The Robert Frost inscription is quoted in ESS, p. 137. Woodress discusses possible connections between the number of volumes in the Professor's works as opposed to WC's own works, p. 208; Brown reference on Myra Henshawe's model is found on p. 248.

7: *Return to Full Circle*

Bogan quote, in *WCHC*, p. 132. EL gives an account of the Taos visit; also of the genesis of the *Archbishop*, p. 139.

The Novels of Faith — 'Frescos' in the *Archbishop*: see letter to the *Commonweal*, in *OW*, p. 9. The record of WC's experiences with Haltermann, churches, etc. in the Southwest is derived largely from the same letter. Rebecca West comment appears in *WCHC*. The ESS quote appears on pp. 227–8. Letter from WC to Ida Tarbell is cited in Woodress, p. 225. 'Happy mood' is in the *Commonweal* letter, *OW* p. 10. On value of old homes: see *WWC*, pp. 146–7. The description of Charles Cather's death is based upon the account recorded in Woodress, who reports letters of WC to Zoë Akin. The description of the Canadian trip is recorded in EL. Impressions of Quebec society are found in Cross letter, *OW*, p. 15. Quote from Garland's diary appears in Woodress, p. 230. Brown records a good discussion of WC's treatment of the historical characters in *Shadows*, pp. 270–1. Brown quote occurs on p. 286.

Final Weakness, Final Strength — The 'division of power' reference is recorded in ESS, p. 240. On dislike of New York, see ESS, p. 237; Woodress, p. 241. The best account of the WC/Menuhin relationship occurs in EL. Woodress refers to the Carrie Miner Sherwood letter. Diary references are recorded in EL. Record of injuries may be found in EL and Woodress. On Sadie Becker as model for *Lucy Gayheart*, see *WWC*, p. 42; letters reported in Woodress, p. 250. Information on the last years is taken from EL, ESS, Brown and Woodress. The trip to Virginia is recounted in EL, pp. 182–3; a full account of the genesis of *Sapphira* occurs on pp. 180–5. 'The Best Years' appears in *The Old Beauty and Others* (1948).

For WC's final days, see especially EL; also Woodress for supplementary information. WC's obituary, *New York Times*, 25 April 1947. Her tombstone bears an inscription from *My Ántonia*: 'That is happiness, to be dissolved into something complete and great'.

Chronology

1873   7 December: Willa Sibert Cather, christened Wilella, is born in Back Creek Valley, Virginia.

1874   The Charles Cathers move to Willow Shade.

1883   The Charles Cathers move to Webster County, Nebraska; the following year they take a house in the town of Red Cloud.

Willa Cather first encounters the Nebraska prairie: 'It was a kind of erasure of personality'.

1890   Graduates from Red Cloud High School: commencement oration, 'Superstition versus Investigation', states that 'all human history is a record of emigration. . . .'

Enters the University of Nebraska at Lincoln.

1891   March: first published work; her Carlyle essay appears in both the *Hesperian* and the *Nebraska State Journal*.

1892   May: first published fiction; 'Peter' is published in *The Mahogany Tree*.

1893   Cather begins writing for the *Nebraska State Journal*; first column, 'One Way of Putting It', appears 5 November.

1895   June: graduates from university. Begins some part-time newspaper work, some short-story writing.

1896   January: letter from Red Cloud is dated 'Siberia'.

June: Cather moves to Pittsburgh, Pennsylvania, to take editorial position with the *Home Monthly*.

Autumn: begins contributing to the *Pittsburgh Daily Leader*.

1897   Spends summer in Nebraska; resigns from the *Home Monthly*. Returns to Pittsburgh as member of *Leader*

157

staff.

1899	Cather meets Isabelle McClung.
1900	Leaves *Leader*. April: 'Eric Hermannson's Soul' published in *Cosmopolitan*. Freelancing in Washington, DC.
1901	Returns to Pittsburgh and lives at McClung residence. Begins teaching career, first at Central, then at Allegheny High School.
1902	With Isabelle McClung, Cather makes her first trip abroad.
1903	*April Twilights* published. Meets Edith Lewis.
1905	McClure, Phillips and Co. publish *The Troll Garden*.
1906	May: Cather joins *McClure's Magazine*; moves to New York City. Her first major assignment takes her to Boston for most of the next two years; afterwards, she becomes managing editor.
1908	Meets Mrs Fields and Sarah Orne Jewett. November: Sarah Orne Jewett writes 'The Letter'; dies (1909) while Cather is on assignment in London for *McClure's*.
1909	With Edith Lewis, Cather takes apartment at 82 Washington Place.
1910	Meets Elizabeth Shepley Sergeant.
1911	Summer: Completes *Alexander's Bridge*, the first 'first novel'. Autumn: visits Cherry Valley with Isabelle McClung on leave of absence from *McClure's*; she never really returns. Writes 'Alexandra' and 'The Bohemian Girl'.
1912	Houghton Mifflin publish *Alexander's Bridge*. First trip to Southwest to visit brother Douglass. Returns to the McClung's; begins *O Pioneers!* 'The Bohemian Girl' appears in *McClure's*. Cather and Edith Lewis rent apartment on 5 Bank

Street, their home for the next fourteen years.

1913   Meets Olive Fremstad.
        O Pioneers! published.
        Complete break with *McClure's*.
        With Isabelle McClung, she visits her 'roots' in the
            Shenandoah Valley, Virginia.

1914   Germany invades Belgium; First World War breaks
            out in Europe.

1915   Mrs Fields dies.
        Second trip to the Southwest: Mesa Verde, Cliff Pa-
            lace.
        The Song of the Lark published.
        Last Christmas with Isabelle McClung; Cather de-
            vastated by Isabelle's engagement.

1917   American entry into First World War.
        Willa Cather goes to Jaffrey, New Hampshire, to visit
            Isabelle and Jan Hambourg; remains in Shattuck
            Inn for the summer and writes.

1918   *My Ántonia* published.
        First World War ends.

1920   Changes publishers to Alfred A. Knopf, who brings
            out *Youth and the Bright Medusa* the same year: 'She
            seemed quite surprised that I knew her name and
            work'.

1922   'The world broke in two. . .'.
        One of Ours published.
        Visits Grand Manan, New Brunswick, for first time.

1923   *A Lost Lady* published.
        Cather is awarded the Pulitzer Prize for *One of Ours*.

1925   Builds Whale Cove Cottage with Edith Lewis.
        Summer in New Mexico; discovers the Macheboeuf
            diary.
        The Professor's House published.

1926   *My Mortal Enemy* published.

1927   *Death Comes for the Archbishop* published.

	Cather and Edith Lewis move to Grosvenor Hotel, 35 Fifth Avenue, New York.
1928	3 March: Charles Cather dies. Cather travels to Grand Manan via Montreal and Quebec. Virginia Cather suffers stroke.
1930	Travels to France; meets the Menuhin family. Gold Medal award of the American Academy of Arts and Letters for *Death Comes for the Archbishop*. Trips to Quebec and Jaffrey.
1931	*Shadows on the Rock* published. August: Virginia Cather dies. Cather becomes first woman to receive honorary degree from Princeton.
1932	*Obscure Destinies* published. Moves to Park Avenue apartment.
1933	Willa Cather becomes first recipient of the Prix Femina Américaín award for *Shadows on the Rock*.
1935	*Lucy Gayheart* published. Isabelle McClung Hambourg ill; Cather spends much of the year caring for her.
1936	*Not Under Forty* published.
1937	Begins preparation for Houghton Mifflin's Library Edition of *The Novels and Stories of Willa Cather*.
1938	June: Douglass Cather dies. October: Isabelle McClung Hambourg dies. Autumn: Cather goes to Jaffrey, only to find much of the woodland destroyed by hurricane.
1939	Second World War breaks out in Europe. 'There seems to be no future at all for people of my generation.'
1940	*Sapphira and the Slave Girl* published on Cather's 67th birthday.

1941	Last long journey, to California to visit brother Roscoe.
1944	Last public appearance: receives gold medal from National Institute of Arts and Letters.
1945	Completes 'The Best Years'. Roscoe Cather dies.
1947	24 April: Willa Sibert Cather dies in New York City. 'She was never more herself than on the last morning of her life', writes Edith Lewis.

Bibliography

Primary Sources

Whenever possible quotations have been taken from the original versions of Cather's works; otherwise, I have used the most authoritative edition available. The main works published during Cather's own lifetime are listed below in order of publication.

April Twilights, 1903. Republished, edited and with an Introduction by Bernice Slote, Lincoln, U. of Nebraska Press, 1968
The Troll Garden, New York, McClure, Phillips, 1905
Alexander's Bridge, Boston and New York, Houghton Mifflin/ Riverside Press, Cambridge, Mass., 1912, 1922
O Pioneers!, London, Heinemann, 1913. Reprinted London, Virago, 1983
The Song of the Lark, Boston and New York, Houghton Mifflin/ Riverside Press, Cambridge, Mass., 1915. I also used the 1943 edition which contains the Preface Cather wrote for the 1932 revised edition. Reprinted London, Virago, 1982
My Ántonia, Boston and New York, Houghton Mifflin/Riverside Press, Cambridge, Mass., 1918. Reprinted London, Virago, 1980
Youth and the Bright Medusa, London, Heinemann, 1921
April Twilights and Other Poems, London, Heinemann, 1924

In 1922 Cather moved to the New York publishing firm of Alfred A. Knopf, who were to remain her sole publishers for the rest of her life:

One of Ours, 1922
A Lost Lady, 1923
The Professor's House, 1925
My Mortal Enemy, 1926
Death Comes for the Archbishop, 1927
Shadows on the Rock, 1931
Obscure Destinies, 1932
Lucy Gayheart, 1935

163

Not Under Forty, 1936
Sapphira and the Slave Girl, 1940

NB: S.S. McClure's *My Autobiography* (London, John Murray, 1919) should really be listed among Cather's works, as her 'ghosting' of the text is well known.

Posthumous Collections

The Old Beauty and Others, New York, Knopf, 1948

Willa Cather on Writing: Critical Studies on Writing as an Art, Foreword by Stephan Tennant, New York, Knopf, 1953

Writings from Willa Cather's Campus Years, ed. James R. Shively, Lincoln, U. of Nebraska Press, 1950

Willa Cather in Europe, Introduction and Notes by George N. Kates, New York, Knopf, 1956

Five Stories, New York, Vintage Books (a division of Knopf), 1956. Contains an article by Kates on the unfinished Avignon story

Early Stories of Willa Cather, Selected and with a Commentary by Mildred R. Bennett, New York; Dodd, Mead, 1957

The Kingdom of Art. Willa Cather's First Principles and Critical Statements, 1893–1896, Edited with two essays and Commentary by Bernice Slote, Lincoln, U. of Nebraska Press, 1970

The World and the Parish: Willa Cather's Articles and Reviews, 1893–1902, Edited with a Commentary by William M. Curtin, Lincoln, U. of Nebraska Press, 1970

Collected Short Fiction 1892–1912, ed. Virginia Faulkner, Introduction Mildred R. Bennett, Lincoln, U. of Nebraska Press, 1970

Uncle Valentine and Other Stories, ed. Bernice Slote, Lincoln, U. of Nebraska Press, 1973

Miscellaneous

'Nebraska. The End of the First Cycle', *The Nation*, vol. 117, no. 3035, pp. 236–8. May also be found in Ernest Gruening, ed., *The United States. A Symposium*, New York, Boni & Liveright, 1924

Secondary Sources

Because of the vast amount of critical writing that has been devoted to Willa Cather during the forty years since her death, readers interested in pursuing her further should turn first to the excellent bibliographic essay by Bernice Slote, which appears in Jackson R. Bryer, ed., *Sixteen Modern American Authors* (New York, Duke UP, 1973). This essay does an excellent job of describing and evaluating critical material up to the early 1970s.

For the reader's convenience, I have divided the secondary material into two parts: works produced by those who knew Willa Cather, either as close friends or professional acquaintances; and those who never knew her personally. While the former accounts provide valuable insights into Cather as a human being, the objective studies are more useful for their critical evaluations and in the accuracy of their biographical details. Although the Brown/Edel biography is remarkable for the amount of ground that it covers, James Woodress' critical biography is by far the most accurate and comprehensive account of its subject that I have read to date.

Personal Accounts

The Letters of Sarah Orne Jewett, ed. Annie Fields, Boston/New York, Houghton Mifflin/Riverside Press, 1911. Contains three letters to Cather.

Elizabeth Shepley Sergeant, *Fire Under the Andes*, New York, Knopf, 1927. Contains a short essay on Cather.

Burton Roscoe, *A Bookman's Daybook*, New York, Liveright, 1929. Contains accounts of meetings with Cather.

George Seibel, 'Miss Willa Cather from Nebraska', *New Colophon*, vol. II, pt 7, 1949, pp. 193–208.

Elizabeth Shepley Sergeant, *Willa Cather. A Memoir*, Philadelphia/New York, Lippincott, 1953.

Edith Lewis, *Willa Cather Living*, New York, Knopf, 1953.

Willa Cather and Her Critics, ed. James Schroeter, New York, Cornell UP, 1967. Contains articles by interviewers and critics; also part of Elizabeth Moorhead's 'The Novelist', repr. from *These Too Were Here: Louise Homer and Willa Cather*. Moorhead was a friend of Cather during the Pittsburgh years.

Other Secondary Sources

David Daiches, *Willa Cather. A Critical Introduction*, New York, Cornell UP, 1951.

E.K. Brown, completed by Leon Edel, *Willa Cather. A Critical Biography*, New York, Knopf, 1953. Brown corresponded!with Cather, although he never met her.

Mildred R. Bennett, *The World of Willa Cather*, Lincoln, U. of Nebraska Press, 1961. Especially good for the early years in Nebraska.

Dorothy Van Ghent, *Willa Cather*, Minneappolis, U. of Minnesota Press, 1964. No. 36 in the Pamphlets on American Writers series.

Richard Giannone, *Music in Willa Cather's Fiction*, Lincoln, U. of Nebraska Press, 1966.

Grant Overton, *The Women Who Make Our Novels*, New York, Books for Libraries, 1967. First published in 1918.

James Woodress, *Willa Cather — Her Life and Art*, Lincoln, U. of Nebraska Press, 1970.

Dorothy Tuck McFarland, *Willa Cather*, New York, Frederick Unger, 1972.

Five Essays on Willa Cather, ed. John Murphy, North Andover, Mass., Merrimack College, 1972. Contains Slote's 'Secret Web' essay.

Kathleen D. Byrne and Richard C. Snyder, *Chrysalis. Willa Cather in Pittsburgh 1896–1906*, Pittsburgh, Historical Society of W. Pennsylvania, 1980.

[James Woodress's, *Willa Cather. A Literary Life*, Lincoln, U. of Nebraska Press, 1988, appeared while this book was at press.]

Some Related Sources

Semi-Centennial Anniversary Yearbook. University of Nebraska 1869–1919, Lincoln, U. of Nebraska Press, 1919. Contains information about the founding of the university, its courses, structure etc., with some photos of the campus.

Frank Luther Mott, *American Journalism. A History 1690–1960*, New York, Macmillan, 1962.

Harold S. Wilson, *McClure's Magazine and the Muckrakers*, New Jersey, Princeton UP, 1970.

166

Peter Lyon, *Success Story — The Life and Times of S.S. McClure*, New York, Charles Scribner's Sons, 1963.

A note on Willa Cather's letters

Testamentary restrictions prevent the publication of Willa Cather's letters, which are housed in numerous libraries and institutions throughout the United States and are thus not easily available to the scholar or interested reader. Because of this, and because this volume is intended only as an introduction to Cather, I have made use of letters verified through other sources. For those with an interest in going to the originals, however, some principal repositories include: the Willa Cather Pioneer Memorial, Red Cloud; the Nebraska State Historical Society, Lincoln; the Newberry Library, Chicago; the University of Virginia, Charlottesville; the University of Vermont, Burlington; and the Huntington Library in San Marino, California.

Index